Creating EAD-Compatible Finding Guides on Paper

Elizabeth H. Dow

The Scarecrow Press, Inc.
Lanham, Maryland • Toronto • Oxford
2005

SCARECROW PRESS, INC.

Published in the United States of America
by Scarecrow Press, Inc.
A wholly owned subsidiary of
The Rowman & Littlefield Publishing Group, Inc.
4501 Forbes Boulevard, Suite 200, Lanham, Maryland 20706
www.scarecrowpress.com

PO Box 317
Oxford
OX2 9RU, UK

British Library Cataloguing in Publication Information Available

Library of Congress Cataloging-in-Publication Data

Dow, Elizabeth H.
  Creating EAD-compatible finding guides on paper / Elizabeth H. Dow.
    p. cm.
  Includes bibliographical references and index.
  ISBN 0-8108-5166-0 (pbk. : alk. paper)
  1. Archival materials—Abstracting and indexing. 2. Cataloging of archival
materials—Standards. 3. Encoded Archival Description (Document type definition)
4. Information storage and retrieval systems—Archival material. I. Title.

Z695.2.D69 2005
025.3'414—dc22

                                                                    2004024574

To

James P. Tranowski

who made all my EAD dreams come true

Contents

Preface

This book grew out of an idea I had one afternoon in my office in the Special Collections Department of the Bailey/Howe Library at the University of Vermont in the spring of 1999. I had spent some time finishing yet another EAD-encoded inventory to put on the Web and noticed how easily and routinely I could do that. I had acquired the tools, I understood the process, and under normal circumstances, I could do final assembly of one in about twenty to thirty minutes. But getting to that point had taken several years and a huge amount of work. I recognized that I had developed knowledge the hard way. I thought I could save a lot of people a lot of time and agony if I shared what I had learned and suggested that they start creating EAD-compliant paper finding aids. With the semi-annual meeting of the New England Archivists coming in the spring, it occurred to me that I could speak on how to start making your paper finding aids EAD compatible—and I did.

In the spring of 2000, while on sabbatical at the University of South Carolina, I repeated the talk to the South Carolina Archivists Association. In both cases people seemed glad to hear what I had to say. It seemed like it might make a useful "how to" book.

The years since then, during which I developed this idea and book, have seen much change in the world of archival description. The Generalized International Standard for Archival Description (ISAD(G)) has appeared in a revised and fuller form; the RLG *Best Practice Guidelines* have undergone substantial revision; and the International Standard for Archival Authority Records for Corporations, Persons, and Families (ISAAR(CPF)) has come into prominence with the Encoded Archival Context (EAC) publication protocol to support delivery of conformant records on the Web. The Canadian and United States Task Force on Archival Description (CUSTARD) Project has produced *Describing Archives: A Content Standard* (DACS). As I send this book to press, various research projects seek to maximize the use of metadata and a variety of information exchange protocols to make it easier for one collection of archival descriptive data to play well with every other kind—all to help researchers find what they need. You can think of the area of electronic description and exchange of archival data as a construction zone which will produce a lot of noise and dust for some time to come but which will eventually provide a well-working infrastructure for us to use to make our resources known by or available to historical researchers.

While the electronic highways, malls, and skyscrapers remain under construction, some parts of the infrastructure have stabilized. You can count on the essential aspects of ISAD(G), DACS, EAD, and the RLG *Best Practice Guidelines* to remain essentially intact. Undoubtedly we will see modifications and refinements over the next decades, but the essential structure will remain—as will the ISO standards you find recommended here. If you still create your finding aids on paper, you need not worry about the noise and dust coming from the electronic protocol developers. You can focus on creating good clear differentiation of your data elements and on using standards at every turn, knowing that with that in place, your data will convert well. At one time, archives description invited creativity and novelty. No longer. Today it wants you to keep your eyes on the standards and follow them steadfastly.

I intend this book to help you put together an archival finding aid that will convert easily to EAD. While the text references arrangement practices, I do not explain arrangement. I do not even go into depth about the analysis and decisions you engage in as you put together your description. I focus on the information you need to collect, where to put it in relation to the other information, and the standards that relate to it.

The documents that define standards present their information in very precise language and in a highly structured format. If you have experience reading such documents, you know they read pretty quickly. But if you do not have that experience, they can seem impenetrable, in part because they usually do not supply much explanation of the context for the concepts they present. In chapter 4, I strive to provide the context, making the standards more comprehensible.

Acknowledgments

I want to thank my supervisors at the Bailey/Howe Library of the University of Vermont, Connell B. Gallagher, director of Research Collections, and Rebecca Martin, dean of Libraries. The two of them gave me endless support from the very beginning.

Hope Greenberg, of UVM's Computing Center's Department of Academic Computing, and Paul Philbin, of the Bailey/Howe's Systems Department, helped me get a grasp on the technology. Jim Tranowski provided the programming that guaranteed the success of everything Special Collections did with EAD and the Model Editions Partnership extension of the Text Encoding Initiative (MEP-TEI, another story altogether). Finally I want to thank the faithful band of undergraduate students who rekeyed dozens of typed inventories. Though not exciting work, it was important.

Sue Easun, my acquisitions editor at Scarecrow, casually planted the put-it-into-a-book idea in my head as I browsed her exhibit at SAA in 2000.

When it came time to put this book together, I depended again on a student—Alison Arán. Ally did a remarkable job of finding examples—far more than finally made it into the book—and arranging for the permission I needed to publish other folks' work.

I also depended on professional colleagues. When I showed up in the e-mail inboxes of Michael Fox and Kris Keisling of the EAD Working Group, they quickly and generously responded to the questions I had. Jean Dreyden of the CUSTARD project offered invaluable help. My mentor, colleague, and friend from our days at the Sheldon Museum, Polly Darnell, read and re-read manuscripts and offered insightful advice that made this text immeasurably easier for you to read and absorb.

The reviewers to whom my editor sent the manuscript for review did me great service. Though I do not know their names, they do, and I'd like to acknowledge their input. The practitioner gave me hope that the final result would prove beneficial. The academic provided many insightful comments and pushed me in directions I might not have thought to go. To both of you: Thanks—I needed that.

Finally, David Chesnutt—book designer, colleague, friend, and husband: as in every other aspect of my life, he made all the difference.

These and others did everything they could to make this a useful manual. Its weaknesses come from my limitations.

Introduction

Many archivists work in repositories that cannot now consider publishing their inventories in any sort of electronic form; they simply do not have the resources—human, financial, or technological. However, their limited resources have not kept them unaware of the growing use of the Encoded Archival Description (EAD) for publishing inventories and other finding aids on the World Wide Web. In fact, many look forward to the day when their repository will also have a place in the Internet's mega-library of intellectual resources, and they would like to start preparing for that day. If you see yourself among them, this book is for you.

If you know that you will create paper inventories for a long time to come, and you also want to know how to make the change from paper to Web publication as easy as possible, this book is for you.

If you have your doubts about all this EAD stuff, please read the next few pages, which make a case for EAD and why you should bother to make your paper inventories EAD compliant.

First, researchers want finding aids on the Web. A 1999 report written by a task force sponsored by the Council on Library and Information Resources (CLIR) and the American Council of Learned Societies (ACLS) carries this observation in the "Summary of Task Force Meetings":

> The most significant impediment to greater access to manuscript materials is the lack of adequate finding aids, in easily located sites.

> The highest priority, therefore, is to continue to create machine-readable records of manuscript holdings and make those records easily accessible on the Web or on a bibliographical utility.[1]

A statement in the "Synthesis of Proceedings" explained further:

> The North American system of bibliographic utilities is regarded as a strong base on which to continue to build for even better access. This system is based on shared development of, and consistent adherence to, standards of content and format of bibliographic records, and on free access to the vast majority of institutional catalogs and other finding aids. The ACLS-CLIR task forces agreed it is a priority to develop finding aids for materials in all formats and in all media. *Renewed diligence is also needed to ensure consistency in the content and format of finding aids,* even as both the range of media and the volume of data multiply, through rapid developments in the Web environment.[2] (Emphasis added)

The emphasized sentence goes to the heart of this book: in a world which depends heavily on computers to do its finding and sorting, consistency makes all the difference. Projects like the Online Archives of California[3] and the Research Libraries Group's "RLG Archival Resources" union catalog of online archival finding aids[4] have demonstrated the feasibility of creating union databases of electronic finding aids. However, successful databases result from rigorous consistency in both the choice of data found in the record and its presentation to the search engine. Creating EAD-compatible finding aids and using the standards associated with the use of EAD will ensure that your finding aids, after conversion, will slip easily onto the Web and into a database where researchers can find them.

Second, EAD reflects the descriptive standards developed by the international archival community. Researchers, accustomed to working with the features of these international standards, will expect to find them in archival inventories, regardless of their medium of creation. In time researchers will equate the look and feel of an EAD-compliant inventory with the way truly professional modern inventories look. They will have learned to use the standard format efficiently and to rely on its features to speed their discovery of potentially useful documents. An EAD-compliant inventory, even if never converted, will speed researchers' access to documents by meeting those expectations.

Third, the use of EAD has grown and will continue to grow. As of December 2004, the "RLG Archival Resources" database contained 49,500 finding aids from 192 providers, about half of them encoded in EAD.[5] The only alternative for putting finding aids larger than a MARC record on the Web has been HTML. HTML can be made to work, but it does not provide the flexibility or the added "intelligence" of EAD. Because of EAD's greater flexibility and power, it has received widespread acceptance. A study conducted in 2003 at the School of Library and Information Science at Louisiana State University revealed that 25 percent of the jobs advertised beween 1997 and 2002 in *Archival Outlook*, the newsletter of the Society of American Archivists, named EAD skills as either required or desirable.[6]

Fourth, creating EAD compliant inventories will not require a great amount of change in the way you do things now. EAD did not come from nowhere. The committee that developed it did so with an eye on research which demonstrated that, despite a wide variety of idiosyncrasies, collection inventories include a core of similar content areas and structures.[7] Therefore, if you decide to create EAD-compliant inventories, your experienced processors will find that, while they will probably need to make some changes in the way they describe collections, most changes will be minor. New processors can incorporate EAD-think into their training with very little effort—if they have not already received it as part of their training for the job.

As an aside, I'll note that although a wholesale reworking of your current practices does not have to accompany EAD compliance in your finding aids, it could. You could take this opportunity to step back, examine your finding-aid creating process, rethink it completely, and develop new ways to do things based on the profession's newly adopted standards.[8]

Fifth, if your institution has just begun to create inventories, creating paper inventories with EAD in mind will provide you with a structure reflecting the common practices of hundreds of institutions throughout the United States and compliant with the growing international consensus of best practices for describing historical collections. You do not need to invent anything; you need merely to choose from the many possibilities EAD offers to create remarkably useful and versatile finding aids.

Finally, when an opportunity to publish your inventories on the Web comes, it probably will not be free. EAD-compliant paper inventories will assure the least expensive conversion. They will include all the data the conversion process will need and in the format it wants. Setting up paper inventories to meet EAD's requirements initially will speed the conversion process and minimize the cost of it, particularly if you create your paper inventories on computers and have created your word processor files with EAD in mind.

About the Focus

As you read this, you will feel a decided tilt to the world of manuscripts and paper. You will feel it for two reasons. One, I came out of the world of manuscripts. I've worked in several repositories and the experience provides the images that spring to my mind in any given situation. Two, I expect that the members of the audience for this small manual more likely work in small manuscript repositories than large government or corporate archives. By extension, I expect they work more with paper than electronic records, and so I focus on paper documents. On the other hand, describing electronic documents differs little in fundamental principles from describing paper documents; description is an area in which electronic records don't need special attention.

I do not think the book's obvious grounding in manuscripts makes it invalid for government or corporate archives. I acknowledge that those archivists will find themselves translating certain terms from the language of manuscript repositories to the language of archives, and I apologize for that inconvenience. After the translation, however, I expect institutional archivists will find the concepts valid.

Another bias appears around the issue of how repositories create new inventories. This book assumes word processing. A fair number of repositories have developed databases for inventory data, and they print paper finding aids from them. Having done that myself, I'm generally aware of the wide variety of database software available for the task, and I decided not to venture off in that direction, lest I never return. Creating a database requires that you really tear your finding aids apart—at least conceptually. I suspect that people developing databases understand the basic principles of data differentiation and controlled access points and have probably already applied them. If they find issues here they have not considered, they have the skill and understanding for translating them into their databases.

A Few Words

A word about EAD versions: This book reflects EAD Version 2002, which has superceded EAD Version 1.0. As a result, it may offer, or appear to offer, guidance contrary to that found in earlier publications. The savvy archivist will adopt the newer standards.

A word about the word "archives." Like many terms in the English language, "archives" has several meanings. In conversational use, people generally rely on context to deduce the meaning; if we cannot deduce the meaning, we ask for clarification. When reading a published work, the reader can not ask for clarification, so the author should pick a meaning and stick with it. In this work, the term "archives" will refer to those materials of enduring value collected by an institution to document its own history. It therefore refers to governmental archives and various forms of organizational and corporate archives. The term "manuscript collections" will refer to personal and family papers. "Historical repositories" will refer to organizations which collect historical documents, be they archives or manuscript repositories.

A word about the word "collection." In archival circles, the term "collection" may also have several meanings. In this work, the term "collection" or "collections," when part of the title in an example, it will mean a group of materials consciously brought together by a collector. Otherwise it will serve as the generic term for aggregates of documents of enduring value. You can depend on the context to indicate the meaning in any given use. Collections of "papers" will refer to those materials connected to the life of individual people or families, and "records" will refer to those materials connected to the history and activity of an organization of any variety. The term "holdings" will refer to the materials—books, collections, non-print materials, etc.—held by a repository.

About Examples

Teaching always requires providing examples of the desired knowledge or behavior, and books like this rely heavily on examples to clarify the rules. In this case, that presents a problem. A few of the rules promoted here are so new that finding examples of recommended practices proved to be a challenge. To fill in gaps, we turned to our imagination. When we use an actual record as an example, we have identified the repository that provided it and we have retained the text as it appears in the original. When we could not find one, we created examples from either the Fictitious Family Papers or the Fictitious College Records. We also used the Fictitious collections as efficient ways to demonstrate several principles, even when real examples exist.

Reading marked-up text takes some getting used to. Lest you get hopelessly confused by the markup and lose the point under discussion, nearly all the examples of markup in this book show only the tagging needed to illustrate the point; an actual document would contain a great deal more. Further, the book does not discuss the entire EAD tag set; it sticks to those tags that relate to essential content elements.

Notes

1. Council on Library and Information Resources, "Scholarship, Instruction, and Libraries at the Turn of the Century," Report no. 78 (January 1999), 15. www.clir.org/pubs/reports/pub78/pub78.pdf.

2. Ibid., 3.

3. www.oac.cdlib.org.

4. www.rlg.org/arr/index.html.

5. Gregory Whitfield, RLG Product Manager, in a private e-mail correspondence to the author, November 23, 2004.

6. Michelle Riggs, "Correlation of Demand for EAD in the Job Market and Graduate Archival Education." Independent study, Fall 2003.

7. Daniel V. Pitti, "Encoded Archival Description: The Development of an Encoding Standard for Archival Finding Aids." *American Archivist* 60:1 (Summer 1997), 268–283.

8. Clay Redding makes a strong case for this approach in his article, "Reengineering Finding Aids Revisited: Current Archival Descriptive Practice and Its Effect on EAD Implementation," *Journal of Archival Organization* 1:3 (2002), 35–50.

Chapter 1

Archival Description: Changing with the Times

History

How can the holder of historically valuable collections make researchers aware of the physical and intellectual contents of those collections? The question has bedeviled archivists from the beginning of the profession. To address it, archivists at many times and in even more places have invented finding aids that worked at the time and place of invention. The generic term "finding aids" has come to encompass a great variety of formats.[1] The genre includes directories of repositories, catalogs of holdings by a repository, and various ways of describing the content of a specific repository. It also includes a wide range of levels of description, such as regional directories to item-level calendars. The examples below reflect the various types of finding aids—in these cases, all published; they also reflect a wide range of coverage—by subject matter, by researcher type, and by geographic region.

Chandler, Marion C. *Colonial and State Records in the South Carolina Archives: A Temporary Summary Guide*. Columbia: South Carolina Department of Archives and History, 1973.

Forbes, Harriette Merrifield. *New England Diaries, 1602–1800, A Description of Diaries, Orderly Books and Sea Journals*. [Topsfield, Ma.] Priv. Print, 1923.

Foster, Janet. *British Archives: A Guide to Archive Resources in the United Kingdom*. New York: Macmillan, 1995.

Neagles, James C. *Locating Your Immigrant Ancestor: A Guide to Naturalization Records*. Logan, Utah: Everton Publishers, 1986.

University of Southwestern Louisiana. *Guide to Southwestern Archives and Manuscript Collection.* Lafayette, La.: The Archives, 1977.

Until recently, highly idiosyncratic archival finding aids met a vital need and posed no problem. Since every collection of original materials in every historical repository had no duplicate in another repository, repositories gained no economy of scale in standardizing the way they described their holdings; they gained no benefit in trying to reuse each other's description of a collection. Doing the enormous amount of work involved in developing and disseminating description standards provided the profession no real gain. Consequently, researchers learned to use the finding aids presented them, regardless of form. No archivist had to explain why the finding aids in his or her repository differed from everyone else's.

In 1980, a literature review and survey done by Elaine Engst at the request of the SAA's newly formed National Information Systems Task Force (NISTF) confirmed a growing awareness that, while the look and feel of the finding aids in institutional archives and manuscript repositories varied widely, the information they included did not. While one repository relied on a card file, another on an inventory, and a third on a calendar, all included the same essential information about the contents of a collection, the context of its creation, and the people involved with it. The level of detail differed dramatically, but the nature of the information did not.[2]

NISTF had requested the report as part of its study of the possibility that the archival community could develop standard ways of organizing finding aid information and standard ways of expressing it to make it amenable to automation. The advent of computers had made that highly desirable. As online public access catalogs (OPACs) in libraries and bibliographic and full-text databases of all sorts became increasingly available to researchers of published material, the perceived value of computer-searchable collections and union databases of archival finding aids grew. Engst's report confirmed the feasibility.

The NISTF report recognized that the cataloging protocol contained in the Machine Readable Cataloging (MARC) format libraries had adopted a decade earlier had proved highly successful. It recommended the development of a MARC format for archives and manuscripts. The new MARC format, labeled MARC for Archival and Manuscript Control (MARC-AMC),[3] while not a perfect vehicle for archival description, promised to make collections intellectually accessible through libraries' online catalogs.[4]

Though many archivists expressed deeply-held doubts that their descriptive practices would fit into a prescribed format,[5] MARC-AMC achieved wide acceptance in the archival community in the United States. MARC had limitations, however. While a cataloger could create a number of records for any one collection (one for the collection as a whole, one for each of the series within a collection, and one for any number of especially important items), the computer could not easily show how these records related to one another. Regardless, when MARC-AMC records joined the millions of bibliographic records available through the OPACs in hundreds of libraries, researchers happily started to find collections they had not known existed.

European repositories, however, did not adopt the use of MARC records for historical collections nearly as widely as American repositories did. Haworth suggests that MARC's inability to display the hierarchical nature of most archival description caused the reluctance. Hensen speculates that the cultural gap between the European library and archives communities may have had an effect.[6] Regardless of the reason, the situation exists. However, although the Europeans did not adopt this early American attempt to standardize archival description, the international archival community did move to adopt standards.

As a worldwide understanding of the need for standards grew, their development took on specifically national perspectives. In the English-speaking world alone, the United States adopted Hensen's *Archives, Personal Papers, and Manuscripts* (APPM) in 1993, Canada adopted the *Rules for Archival Description* (RAD) in 1990, and Great Britain adopted the *Manual of*

Archival Description (MAD) in 1986. All focused on different issues with rec-
ommendations that varied, assuring that the resulting records differed from
slightly to conspicuously. Recognizing that everyone's data must work together for effective international access and retrieval of archival finding aids,
the International Council of Archivists (ICA) adopted a set of general principles for the description of archival materials in the early 1990s; they called
it the Generalized International Standard for Archival Description, abbrevi-
ated to ISAD(G). The council adopted the second edition in 1999—
ISAD(G)v2.

Close on the heels of ISAD(G) came the World Wide Web, which created
the possibility of electronic publishing of full archival finding aids for the
whole world to use—if a protocol for doing it could be developed. The idio-
syncracies of archival descriptive practices, which had once seemed so charm-
ingly quaint, emerged as a barrier to the intellectual access of historical collections in an era when scholars started to look first to the World Wide Web
for information.[7]

While the ICA started disseminating standard descriptive practices, Daniel
Pitti headed up a project at the Bancroft Library at the University of California at Berkeley to develop a way to electronically publish inventories. After
local success, Berkeley approached the SAA for support in refining and en-
dorsing the protocol for general use. The SAA accepted the offer and convened an EAD Working Group to turn "FindAid," as the protocol was called
at Berkeley, into Encoded Archival Description (EAD).[8] Michael Fox of the
Minnesota Historical Society served on both the EAD Working Group
(EADWG) and the ISAD(G) committee. His awareness of ISAD(G) developments and a general intention of the EADWG informed the development of
EAD, although it did not dominate it. Fox had also served on the Machine
Readable Bibliographic Information Committee (MARBI), the regulatory
body for the MARC format. Again, while the EADWG did not organize EAD
to reflect MARC, EAD allows a fairly easy extraction of a MARC record
from its data.

EAD Version 1 officially appeared in 1997.[9] Its adoption by repositories exposed it to situations not tested, and the Working Group quickly developed a list of requests and complaints from new users, including Europeans who asked for closer conformance to ISAD(G). In response to that early reaction, the committee immediately started a revision which it released as EAD Version 2002. Version 2002 conforms closely to ISAD(G)v2; more on ISAD(G)v2 in chapter 2.

In 2001, the Society of American Archivists received funding to support the Canadian-United States Task Force on Archival Description, immediately dubbed CUSTARD, in an effort to develop a North American standard for archival description. CUSTARD resulted in major revisions of the basic archival descriptive guidelines used by both nations. Canada moved from RAD to RAD2; the United States moved from Hensen's APPM to *Describing Archives: A Content Standard* (DACS); more about DACS in chapter 2.

Thinking about Archival Description

Before diving into all these descriptive standards, let's step back a moment and reflect on what archival description wants to accomplish. We usually think of "description" as half of the team of "arrangement and description." The "arrangement" half represents the physical and intellectual ordering of archival materials—the way we put the materials in folders, boxes, drawers, shelves, etc. "Description" represents our efforts to convey the intellectual and physical content to users, whether researchers or repository staff. When we arrange archival materials, we seek to create order. When we describe, we seek to convey to potential users some sense of the content and the intellectual relationships that exist within the materials. Since the late twentieth century, archivists have focused more and more on good description because they have come to understand that the best arrangement in the world means little if its description does not consistently and accurately describe the collection, facilitate efficient retrieval of relevant materials, adhere to and contribute to the growing body of authority data, and integrate well with other modern archival descriptions. The physical manifestation of the descriptive process has come to be known as a finding aid.

A Closer Look at Finding Aids

All finding aids serve both the repository staff and the researcher in the reading room. A repository's collection of finding aids helps staff keep track of their institution's holdings by showing where they came from, what state they are in, where to find them, and what restrictions might apply to them. A finding aid provides the researcher with a document which describes one or more collections in more or less detail so she or he will know what portions might hold useful information. A finding aid serves as both an administrative tool and as an information retrieval tool. As an information retrieval tool, they serve first at the intellectual level, and then at the physical level.

Inventories

Inventories, also called registers by the National Archives, have become the professional standard for describing archives and manuscript collections. They consist of a general narrative description of the entire collection followed by more detailed summary descriptions of component series, if any. Following these larger prose areas comes a listing of the containers—boxes and folders—presented in a way that reflects their intellectual order and container type. Individual items may also have a listing, although not usually. The example of an older finding aid on the next page describes a two-box collection. One box holds six volumes which it names; the other box holds three volumes and six folders.

Special Collections, Bailey/Howe Library, University of Vermont:
   East Charlotte Baptist Church, East Charlotte, Vermont
   2 Boxes
   Bound Volumes and Manuscripts, 1882–1943
   The church was organized in Charlotte, May 6, 1807, by 19 members

released from the church in Monkton, Vermont, for this purpose. In October of 1807, the church united with the Vermont Association convened in Bridport, and in 1834 with the Addison Association.

Box 1   Volume
          1 Horsford Library Record Book; 1800's–1900's
          2   "   "   "   "   ; 1907–1923
          3 Ladies Aid Society: Financial Records; 1898–1936
          4 " "   " : Records; 1902–1931
          5 " "   " : Records; 1931–1937
          6 Women's Missionary Society: Book of Records; 1908–1919

Box 2   Volume
          1 Sunday School Records: Roll Book; 1903–1906
          2 Treasurer's Book: Records; 1882–1896
          3   "   " : Contributions Received; 1896–1908

Folder
   1 Clerk's Letter File: Correspondence; 1884–1940
   2   "   "   " : Membership Letters; 1884–1938
   3   "   "   " : Church Statistics; 1893–1919
   4   "   "   " : Meetings and Reports; 1906–1942
   5   "   "   " : Annual Report to Vermont Baptist
                        State Convention; 1923–1939
   6   "   "   " : Church Executive Committee; 1940–1943

Calendars

Calendars get their names from the fact that they typically provided a chronological list of documents, frequently with an abstract noting type of document, creator, date and place of creation, the page or leaf count, and a summary of the contents like the calendar of letters example below. Researchers find calendars highly valuable, but they require an enormous amount of effort to produce.

Special Collections, Bailey/Howe Library, University of Vermont:
Colonel Isaac Clark, 1749–1822
Papers, 1781–1821
One box

Background

Isaac Clark, (1749–1822) of Castleton, Vermont, served in both the American Revolution and the War of 1812....A hero of the American Revolution, he participated in the Battle of Bennington on August 16, 1777, and the re-capture of Fort Ticonderoga in 1778. Clark married Governor Thomas Chittenden's daughter, Hannah, in 1779....

Isaac Clark is best known for his leadership of the Vermont troops during the War of 1812. His responsibilities as Colonel of the 11th Infantry, Champlain District, included patrolling the Quebec/Vermont border to prevent the lucrative smuggling trade throughout the conflict, and he led several forays into lower Quebec in 1813 and 1814....

Collection Description

The Colonel Isaac Clark Papers consist primarily of personal and military correspondence from 1812–1821. Clark's letters relate to troop activity in the Champlain Valley.... The Papers also contain materials pertaining to political issues before and after the War of 1812. The Papers are arranged chronologically.

Box 1

Folder	Contents	Date
7	Truman Galusha, ALS to Gen. Isaac Clark. 2 pp., re: family matters (Clark's nephew)	Oct. 20, 1811
8	S. [Satterlee] Clark, ALS to Father (Clark).	Nov. 15, 1811

3 pp., from Annapolis; on family matters and
national politics; news of the impending war.
   (with typescript)

9 Lt. Satterlee Clark; ALS to Father.   Feb. 7, 1812
   3 pp., from Annapolis; I. Clark has been recommended
   for U. S. Army Commission as Brigadier-General;
   brief mention of Gen. Harrison at Tippecanoe.

10 Lt. V.R. Goodrich, ALS to Col. Clark.   June 5, 1812
   1 p., from Swanton; reports on the opening of
   recruiting station at that post.

11 Sen. Jonathan Robinson, ALS to Col. Clark.   June 9, 1812
   1 p., from Washington; announces "the die is cast,"
   declaration of war will be made public in 10 days.
      (with typescript)

Lists

Lists disclose an institutions' holdings of a well-known type of material,
such as a list of holdings of newspapers, *cartes de visites*, annual reports, etc.
Lists may describe the contents of an entire collection, for example, a list of
images in a photograph collection, or a portion of a collection, such as the
images in an otherwise largely manuscript collection. Repositories also use
lists to create easy intellectual access to an array of their holdings that have
some commonality, like the list on the next page.

Louisiana and Lower Mississippi Valley Collections, Special Collections, LSU Libraries:

Manuscript Resources on the Sugar Industry

This guide describes manuscript collections documenting the sugar industry in the Louisiana and Lower Mississippi Valley Collections (LLMVC) at LSU. The records and personal papers of sugar planters and others whose livelihood came from growing sugar provide a wealth of documentation supporting research in agriculture, sociology, economics, history, and politics.

A. Ledoux, Miltenberger and Hall Company. Account book, 1856–1857. 1 vol. (110 pages, 62 l.); 36.3 cm. Location: W:53. Plantation record book kept by Samuel Leigh and Lewis F. Pulliam, overseers of the sugar plantation owned by A. Ledoux and Company, Pointe Coupee Parish, Louisiana. Available on microfilm: UPA Records of Ante-bellum Southern Plantations Series I, Part 1, Reel 9. For further information see online catalog. Mss. 964.

Allyn, William B. Letter, 1862 Nov. 25. 1 item. Location: Misc:A. William B. Allyn was a Federal officer serving in Louisiana during the Civil War. Written from Camp Stevens, near Thibodaux, Lafourche Parish, Louisiana, Allyn's letter describes the surrounding countryside, the Federal policy toward captured Confederate sugar, and social relations with local planters. For further information see online catalog. Mss. 2941.

Ashland Plantation record book, 1852. 1 vol. Location: M:19. W. C. Wade was an overseer of the Ashland Plantation, Ascension Parish, Louisiana. Ashland Plantation was owned by the sugar planter and politician, Duncan Farrar Kenner (1813–1887). The record book contains daily entries which describe activities on the Ashland Plantation. Available on microfilm: UPA Records of Ante-bellum Southern Plantations

Series I, Part 1, Reel 13. For further information see online catalog. Mss. 534.

Carroll, Daniel R. Family papers, 1870–1948. 191 items, 1 ms. vol. Location: T:6, Vault. Owner of Ackbar Plantation, Jefferson Parish, Louisiana. Carroll was also a cotton broker in New Orleans. Papers include personal letters, scrapbooks, and genealogies of the Carroll and Parker families. Some papers document plantation management, including sugarcane growing, rice planting, the construction of a sugar mill, and black laborers. For further information see online catalog. Mss. 1514, 2296.

Indexes

Indexes provide a detailed analysis of a collection or group of related collections. Typically indexes include location information. For example, an institution might create an index of correspondents in a collection of the papers of a prominent person whose correspondence contains works by a wide variety of people that might interest researchers.

The University of Vermont's "George Percival Auld Papers: Index of Correspondents" lists author and recipient, date, occasionally a subject, and the box-folder location; no number under the location implies a ditto mark.

[Sroles, P.] to [G.P.A.]	1/25/23	6-4
Stearns, Joseph T. to N.Y. Bd. Regents	4/6/26	G.P.A
Steiner, Frederick f[rom] F.D.R.	4/8/35	6-1
Sterrett, J. E. to G.P.A.	3/29/20	
" f "	2/18/22	
" to "	8/23/26	
" to Sec'y. of Navy	1/12/20	G.P.A. 9-5

MARC Records

MARC records of archival materials commonly appear in online public ac
cess catalogs holding a brief description of either a collection or a collection'
finding aid. As part of an electronic database, the record gives the compute
a variety of controlled-language fields to search including names of people
corporations and places, genres, occupations, and topical subject headings
MARC records also include text fields for historical context and the scop
and content of the collection. When describing collections, a MARC record
which averages about 750 printed characters, may summarily describe larg
collections which have extensive additional finding aids. It may also serv
as the sole finding aid for one- or two-folder sized collections. Finally, it ca
treat a finding aid as a discrete publication and describe it without describ
ing the collection per se.

Vermont Archival Network, ARCat:
Vermont. Governor (1977–1985 : Snelling)
Abenaki Indians : records, 1976–1983.
10 folders.

The Vermont Commission on Indian Affairs was created in November 1976 as an advisory commission. In January 1977 it was modified to
some degree.

Correspondence, memos and reports on the Abenaki's attempts to
gain status in Vermont and on the Vermont Commission on Indian Af-
fairs, which was established by Snelling's executive order #3.
Abenaki Indians—Vermont.
Clippings.
Executive orders.
Letters.
Memoranda.
Snelling, Richard A.
Salmon, Thomas P.

Vermont. Commission on Indian Affairs.

Abenaki Tribal Council.

Office of the Secretary of State, Vermont State Archives, 26 Terrace St., Montpelier, Vt. 05609–1103

Vermont Archival Network, ARCat:

Ladies Domestic Missionary Society (Middlebury, Vt.)

Records, 1870–1902.

1 folder.

The Ladies Domestic Missionary Society was a group of women from the Congregational Church of Middlebury who organized to support domestic (as opposed to foreign) missions and began contributing money to the Vermont Domestic Missionary Society between 1800 and 1810.

Annual reports, including names of officers and amount of annual contributions to the Vermont Domestic Missionary Society; and other papers. Includes notes and a letter relating to the history of the Vermont society.

Church societies—Vermont—Middlebury.

Home missions—Societies, etc.

Women—Vermont—Societies and clubs.

Women in charitable work—Vermont.

Vermont Domestic Missionary Society.

Sheldon Museum, Middlebury, Vt. 05753.

Sometimes all types appear in the description of one collection. Over the course of the stewardship of several curators, a large, important, and complicated collection may inspire the creation of several types of finding aids as the needs for various types of information arise. The collection of a long-term elected official, for instance, might first receive a general inventory. Finding the inventory long and cumbersome to work with, the curator might create an index of correspondents, a list of committee appointments, a calendar of speeches, and make available whatever devices the official's staff kept for their own use of the papers.

Common Elements

Regardless of their differences, most finding aids provide similar types of information:

1. A title which the archivist has supplied to connect the finding aid to the creator of the collection;
2. A summary description of the material described in the finding aid;
3. Background and context of the collection, its creator, and the major figures involved; and
4. Information about the custodial history of the collection in question, and any restrictions and conditions that apply to its use. It may include much more.

For all their similarities, however, finding aids vary widely in their structure, their completeness of detail, the order in which information appears, and the type and format of additional information, such as chronological lists, lists of important correspondents, specific elements of the collection (e.g., an index of speeches in a political collection), etc. Moving from collection to collection within a single repository and then from repository to repository, one can readily see why the notion of "standardizing" archival description met resistance.

Since the inventory has become the basic finding aid for manuscript repositories, this book will use the language of inventories. The reader should know, however, that EAD will support other formats.

Notes

1. Steven L. Hensen, " 'NISTF II' and EAD: The Evolution of Archival Description," *American Archivist* 60 (Summer 1997): 286.

2. Elaine Engst, "Standard Elements for the Description of Archives and Manuscript Collections: A Report to the Society of American Archivists Task Force on National Information Systems." [September 1980]. Photocopy in the possession of the author.

3. Hensen, 286–287.

4. In 1988–1989, MARBI voted to integrate the eight MARC bibliographic tag sets developed for a variety of formats (books, serials, maps, visual materials, archives and manuscripts, computer files, sound recordings, and scores) into a single expanded set known as USMARC. USMARC retained the fields and protocols developed for archival description. Walt Crawford, *MARC for Library Use*, 2nd ed. (Boston: G.K. Hall, 1989): 209.

5. Hensen, 290.

6. Kent M. Haworth, "Archival Description: Content and Context in Search of Structure," in Daniel V. Pitti and Wendy Duff, eds., *Encoded Archival Description on the Internet* (New York: Haworth, 2001), 20; Steven L. Hensen, "Archival Cataloging and the Internet: The Implications and Impact of EAD," in Daniel V. Pitti and Wendy Duff, eds., *Encoded Archival Description on the Internet* (New York: Haworth, 2001), 82.

7. In 1997 I worked at the reference desk in the Special Collections Department of the Bailey/Howe Library at the University of Vermont. A graduate student approached me one day, seeking guidance on using the holdings. He had reached the thesis point in his program, and had come to Special Collections looking for inspiration on a topic and the materials with which to research it. I pointed out the thirty-drawer card catalog which provided some intellectual access to smaller collections and roughly ten linear feet of loose-leaf notebooks holding inventories. I suggested that he start by browsing certain areas in those two resources. He glanced at the card catalog and finding aids and turned back to me. Looking clearly put off by what he had just seen, he said "I don't do that. I'll get something I can find on the computer."

8. Daniel V. Pitti, "Encoded Archival Description: The Development of an Encoding Standard for Archival Finding Aids," *American Archivist* 60 (Summer 1997): 268–283.

9. Two special issues of *American Archivist* described and explained the protocol. *American Archivist* 60 (Summer 1997): 264–354, and 60 (Fall 1997): 370–455. At the same time, the SAA made the technical files available on its website for downloading.

Chapter 2

ISAD(G)v2 and DACS

MARC-AMC proved useful but inadequate.[1] MARC provided a format for creating a brief description that could apply at the collection level, the series level, or the item level, but it lacked the detail and robustness needed to describe collections as fully as the old-fashioned finding aids. Its adoption and use, however, demonstrated that archivists could standardize the way they described their holdings. That awareness supported efforts in the late 1980s to define what a universal standard for archival description should include. The International Council on Archives (ICA) charged its Committee on Descriptive Standards to analyze current practice and create a data structure to serve as the basis for international standardization of archival description.

In 1994 the ICA announced the General International Standard Archival Description, known as ISAD(G); a revised second edition appeared in 1999.[2] ISAD(G)v2 represents the agreed-on data elements and basic structure that the international archival community applies to describing archival materials. The EAD Working Group has consciously brought EAD into alignment with ISAD(G)v2. Therefore, you can start to understand EAD by becoming familiar with ISAD(G)v2.

A Word about Information Data Labels

All archivists use four data-related concepts as they create finding aids but most probably have not labeled them as such. Before we go further, let's look at the concepts and apply the labels information specialists typically use: data element, data value,[3] data structure, and data format.

First, when you get down to processing a collection, you know what you want to know about it: who created it, who owned it, what years it covers, what sources and information it contains, etc. In the information world, those questions reflect the *data elements* you seek. ISAD(G)v2 defines the data elements needed for a full description of a collection of historical documents. It tells you what information to include in your description.

Next, knowing what data elements you want to collect, you turn to the issue of where to find them. Undoubtedly your institution has a standard procedure for choosing a collection's creator, tracing its history, determining the dates it covers, etc. That procedure will tell you where to look and what to choose as the relevant information. In the information world, those procedures will get the *data values* you need. They will give you the actual information. ISAD(G)v2 says almost nothing about data value.

Then, when you locate the information, you may fill out a form which instructs you to put certain information in certain places. The forms provide a *data structure* for you to fill in. They label a data element (e.g., date) and provide you space for entering the data value you have collected. The forms assure that you will always put the same data value in the same place in the data structure. The regularity they provide makes forms very convenient for a lot of purposes. For instance, because you know that certain information will always appear at a specific place on a page, you know where to put your eyes. Further, forms serve as reminders of the information you need to collect. ISAD(G)v2 provides a general guide to the data structure archival description should adhere to.

Finally, forms serve another purpose in that they frequently prompt you to provide data in the proper *data format*. For instance, you may discover that a small collection holds minutes from meetings held between January 10, 1935 and March 8, 1936. You have many options for the way you might format those dates: Jan. 10, 1935–March 8, 1936; 1/10/1935–3/8/1936; 10/

1/1935–8/3/1936; 1935/01/10–1936/03/08, etc. ISAD(G)v2 says almost nothing about data format.

Summary

- Data element refers to the points of information you collect.
- Data value refers to the specific information for each element.
- Data structure refers to where you put the data value.
- Data format refers to how you present the data value.

Data Value and Format

ISAD(G)v2 details the various data elements you need. It does not say where to find that information or how to format it. It establishes twenty-six separate data elements which all archival description could contain. For instance, ISAD(G)v2 requires that every collection's description should indicate a creator for the collection, but it does not dictate how the archivist should choose the creator among several plausible candidates. Nor does it say how that creator's name should appear in the actual finding aid. Of the twenty-six, ISAD(G)v2 lists six data elements that must appear. It promises that taken together those six will assure the collection a unique identity in all the world.

ISAD(G)v2 also defines how various elements should relate to one another—the data structure—whether recorded on paper or in an electronic file. It does *not* include either what particular information the archivist should use (data value) or how to format it (data format) in the description. To summarize: ISAD(G)v2 defines data elements and a data structure, but it does not define the data value or the data format of the description; it leaves these to local or national standards and practice.

Until the publication of *Describing Archives: A Content Standard*,[4] American archivists turned to *Archives, Personal Papers and Manuscripts* by Steve Hensen[5] for guidance on data value and format. Canadians turn to *Rules for Archival Description* by the Canadian Council of Archivists.[6]

There is nothing revolutionary about ISAD(G)v2. It merely articulates and refines what has become common practice among archivists in an attempt to reduce idiosyncrasies of description by identifying the commonalities in descriptive practices all over the world. The explanation below attempts to draw attention to those ISAD(G)v2-supported practices that relate most closely to converting a paper finding aid to EAD markup. A number of books on archival arrangement and description exist on the market, and the reader should not think that this small chapter will replace any one of them.[7]

As mentioned above, ISAD(G)v2 defines a broad data structure for at least the conceptual arrangement of the collection and usually for the actual physical arrangement as well.[8] Specifically:

1. As much as possible, repositories should keep records an organization or person created, accumulated, and/or maintained in their original order. In other words, a repository must not mix or combine one collection's materials with other collection's materials, regardless of the subject matter or people involved. This means that no matter how the repository houses its collections, its records must make clear the origins and history (the provenance) of each collection, so a researcher may locate all the material the repository holds from a single creator.[9] For example:

Fictitious College Records, 1889–1942. 10 linear feet, 6 volumes. Administrative records of Fictitious College, founded by Fearless Leader Fictitious.

Fictitious Family Papers, 1850–1998. 15 linear feet, 12 volumes. Papers of three generations of the Fictitious Family, including Fearless L. Fictitious, his wife Malvina, their son, Cornelius, his wife Eleanora Hay Fictitious, and their daughter, Sue Ann Fictitious.

Although the individuals in these two collections overlap, the physical collections and the description of them must not.

2. When processing collections, archivists should arrange materials according to a system of hierarchical levels which give priority to the intellec-

tual relationships within the collection. After finishing the physical arrangement, the repository should describe a collection in a way that reflects the conceptual hierarchical arrangement.[10]

Obviously many very small collections (e.g., a few folders of correspondence between just two people) do not require an elaborate hierarchical description. However, when collections naturally break into segments, archival principles say that an archivist should recognize those breaks and use them to establish a set of levels that nest together, like one or more sets of Russian dolls.

Each inventory will refer to only one collection, for example the Fictitious Family Papers or the Fictitious College Records. Collections represent an actual physical collection of materials which may divide into a number of smaller units. We can represent these levels and the way they relate to one another by thinking of them as an outline.[11]

Below the collection level (i.e., the top or all-encompassing level), a collection will divide into a number of series. Materials in a series share a common characteristic that gives them their identity as a series. The characteristics vary widely. A series may share a common physical make-up such as maps or photo albums; it may represent a period of time, such as affiliation with a particular part of the creator's career or stage of life or the administration of a particular officer over an organization; they may also represent a function within an institution, such as the records of the human resources department. Depending on the size of a collection or series, the archivist may also find subcollections and subseries. For example:

Fictitious Family, 1850–1999 [Collection]
    Fearless L. and Malvina T. Fictitious [Subcollection]
    Cornelius J. and Eleanora H. Fictitious
    Sue Ann Fictitious
      Education [Series]
        Fictitious College, 1961–1965 [Subseries]

        Rainy University, 1969–1970
        Snowy University, 1979–1985
        Smokey University, 1983–1988
    Careers

Fictitious College, 1887–1943 [Collection]
    Office of the President, 1889–1942 [Subcollection]
        Administration of Fearless Leader Fictitious, 1889–1929 [Series]
            Public Relations Materials, 1889–1900 [Subseries]
            Financial Data, 1889
        Administration of Cornelius J. Fictitious, 1929–1942
    Office of the Dean of Students, 1889–1942

Despite the level of complexity of the series structure, the *file* level will follow. The file level describes the smallest aggregate of materials within a collection, holding documents grouped together by the creator or processor because they reflect a specific subject, activity, genre, etc. A file may hold any number of individual folders. The folders in a file usually have the same name and serve only to physically house the materials. The file imposes an intellectual order on the materials.

The fourth level, the *item* level, refers to the smallest unit of all, for example, a document or record.

Fictitious Family [Collection]
    Sue Ann Fictitious [Subcollection]
        Education [Series]
            Fictitious College, 1961–1965 [Subseries]
            Rainy University, 1969–1970
            Snowy University, 1979–1985

Papers, 1979–1980 [Sub-subseries]

Thesis, 1980–1986 [Sub-sub-subseries]
Drafts, 1983–1986 [File]
Manuscript notes, 1979–1983
Monograph notes, 1980–1983
Newspaper notes, 1978–1983
Oral history notes, 1980–1983
Final draft, 1986 [Item]
Smokey University, 1983–1988
Careers [Series]

Clearly the intellectual description in an inventory will relate to the physical arrangement. Therefore, inventories which an archivist builds as part of processing a collection cannot reach final form until the processing of the collection has finished. However, the savvy archivist works out the intellectual and the physical arrangement in stages. By starting with a general survey of the collection, the archivist can develop—on paper—a conceptualization of the collection's arrangement, largely reflecting the original order of the collection as it came into the repository. By doing the original conceptualization on paper, the archivist can save a lot of time and handling of materials. While mindful of original order, she or he adjusts the components on paper until the arrangement seems to makes sense. At that point the archivist can start moving actual materials. As processing proceeds, however, the archivist will discover that the paper conceptualization, regardless of how well done, will need repeated adjustment to respond to realities of the collection. While the conceptual arrangement and explanatory notes form the basis of the finding aid, the document will remain in flux to the very end. The physical arrangement process always ends before the descriptive process.

3. Given the multilevel nature of archival description, the archivist should present the information from the most general to the most specific. Going from the general to the specific implies a couple of other practices. First, the

information supplied at any descriptive level applies to the level at which it appears. In other words, the archivist should not supply detailed information about the contents of files when describing the collection or series. Nor should lengthy discussion of the whole collection appear at any lower level.

Second, the information presented at any level should also generally apply to the levels below it. The higher the level of description, the more general and encompassing the information it contains. A description of the Education series below should include information that applies to all the subseries below it and avoid information that applies to only one. It would not include information that relates to Ms. Fictitious's careers. Information that applies to Rainy University only would appear in the notes about that subseries.

Fictitious Family [Collection]
    Sue Ann Fictitious [Subcollection]
    Education [Series]
           Fictitious College, 1961–1965 [Subseries]
           Rainy University, 1969–1970
           Snowy University, 1979–1985
           Smokey University, 1983–1988
    Careers [Series]

Third, the archivist must clearly indicate the relationships between the levels of the collection. That relationship will appear in the language used to describe the levels, but for a visual impression, as in the example above, indentation serves that purpose admirably.

4. The researcher cannot fully understand the context or structure of a collection without knowledge of the principal creators and the provenance of the documents. The archivist must supply this information. Contextual information takes several forms in a finding aid. The biographical (person) or historical (institution) section of the finding aid supplies a

prose description of who, what, where, when, and why about the collection. In the process, the biographical and historical section may include chronological lists, time lines, organizational charts, family trees, and other formalized presentations of supporting information. Regardless of format, the information tells the story that surrounds and explains the creation of the materials it relates to.

Every story has a cast of characters. The finding aid must present them according to the degree of their importance to the creation of the collection and must remove any ambiguity about exactly who is whom, especially in families where names may reappear across generations. The archivist does this most clearly by providing a full name with birth and death information. In the many cases in which those dates remain elusive, providing a date of "flourishing" places the person or organization in time. This contextual history provides the core data on the provenance of the materials and thereby speaks to the authenticity of both the materials and information in them.

Organization

ISAD(G)v2 mandates the use of nested component parts for describing collections. EAD supports it easily. The components may consist of series and their nests of subseries, files, and items. EAD will support nesting to an infinite degree; you can describe as complex a hierarchy of components as the collection requires without fear of creating EAD coding problems at the time of conversion.

Series and subseries arise from some commonality among the contents. That similarity may rest on:

1. physical qualities (genre), for example, a map series, photographs, or bound volumes;
2. document form or function, for example, minutes, land deeds, notes, or business correspondence;
3. creator, for example, an individual family member, a corporate branch, or a corporate officer;
4. time, for example, retirement years, war-time effort, term of a public official; or

    5. place, for example, in a collection of regional records, the
records on each member unit can serve as a series.

Any component may contain a number of other components, arranged according to different qualities, for example, a creator-based series subdivided by time, which in turn is divided by place.

Adhering to the principle of original order, an archivist, especially in a manuscript repository, "discovers" components within a collection and then somewhat artificially establishes boundaries around them. Only when no original order exists does the archivist create an order. In the example below, we see that Sue Ann Fictitious consulted a variety of sources for her thesis work, and the archivist who processed her papers found her notes in one box where Sue Ann had put them without any discernable order. Because so few of the documents indicated a date of creation, the archivist could not arrange them chronologically. Organizing them by source gave the series, and each file in it, a manageable and intelligible coherence.

Fictitious Family [Collection]
   Sue Ann Fictitious [*Creator:* Subcollection]
      Education [*Content:* Series]
         Fictitious College, 1961–1965 [*Time/place*: Subseries]
         Rainy University, 1969–1970
         Snowy University, 1979–1985
            Papers, 1979–1980 [*Genre*: Sub-subseries]
               Thesis, 1980–1986 [*Content*: Sub-sub-subseries]
                  Oral history notes, 1980–1983 [*Content*: File]
                  Newspaper notes, 1978-1983 [*Content*: File]
                  Drafts, 1983–1986 [*Genre*: File]
                     Final draft, 1986 [Item]
         Smokey University, 1983–1988 [*Time/place*: Subseries]
      Careers [*Content*: Series]

The normal record-keeping process of the college determined the series division within its records.

Fictitious College, 1887–1943 [Collection]

   Office of the President, 1889-1942 [*Creator:* Subcollection]

      Administration of Fearless Leader, 1889–1929 [*Time:* Series]

         Public Relations Materials, 1889–1900 [*Content:* Subseries]

         Financial Data, 1889 [*Content:* Subseries]

      Administration of Cornelius J. Fictitious, 1929–1942 [*Time:* Series]

   Office of the Dean of Students, 1889–1942 [*Creator:* Subcollection]

DACS

Describing Archives: A Content Standard (DACS) grew out of the CUSTARD discussions among American and Canadian archivists. It combines the essential role of both ISAD(G) and Hensen's APPM. ISAD(G) identified a set of data elements for inclusion in archival descriptions. APPM explained how to fill in some of the data elements, but not all. APPM came in response to MARC and expanded on the *Anglo-American Cataloging Rules,* 2nd edition[12] used by librarians for cataloging books. As a result, APPM focused heavily on identifying, choosing, and formatting the names of people, places, and corporate entities.

DACS also establishes a set of data elements. It provides guidance on identifying, choosing, and formatting the information that belongs in each element. In addition, DACS provides an example of each element as it might appear in both a MARC record and an EAD instance. In other words, DACS does everything APPM did, and a great deal more. According to the SAA, DACS supercedes APPM.

Notes

1. Daniel Pitti, "Encoded Archival Description: The Development of an Encoding Standard for Archival Finding Aids." *American Archivist* 60 (Summer 1997): 273–276.

2. www.ica.org/eng/work/standards.html.

3. Frequently called *data content*.

4. *Describing Archives: A Content Standard*. (Chicago: Society of American Archivists, 2004).

5. Steven L. Hensen, *Archives, Personal Papers, and Manuscripts: A Cataloging Manual for Archival Repositories, Historical Societies, and Manuscript Libraries* (Chicago: Society of American Archivists, 1998).

6. Popularly known as RAD (1990) and RAD2 (2003) and published by the Canadian Council of Archivists. *Rules for Archival Description* (Ottawa: Canadian Council of Archivists, 2003). www.cdncouncilarchives.ca/archdesrules.html

7. Frederic Miller, *Arranging and Describing Archives and Manuscripts*, (Chicago: Society of American Archivists, 1990); Michael Fox, Peter Wilkerson, and Susan Warren, *Introduction to Archival Arrangement and Description: Access to Cultural Heritage* (Los Angeles: Getty Information Institute, 1998); Michael G. Cook, *The Management of Information from Archives*, 2nd ed. (Burlington, Vt.: Gower Press, 1999); Margaret Procter and Michael G. Cook, *Manual of Archival Description*, 3rd ed. (Burlington, Vt.: Gower Press, 2000); *Rules for Archival Description* (Ottawa: Canadian Council of Archivists, 2003).

8. While, conceptually, certain materials might belong with one group of materials in a collection (e.g., maps with travel journals) for a variety of reasons, the repository might physically store them in a different place. The inventory will reflect the conceptual closeness of these materials as well as their physical distance.

9. The two concepts (i.e., the importance of the provenance of records and their original order), when taken together, make up the concept called *respect des fonds*, meaning essentially to show respect for the collection as an entity unto itself.

10. ISAD(G)v2 officially acknowledges four formal levels that exist within collections, but the committee took that position to avoid having to describe an

endless number of sublevels. Implicitly it recognizes that most collections will have many sublevels of the series level and perhaps the collection level.

11. Institutional records tend to have rather clearly defined boundaries, based on the hierarchy of the institution and job description that tends to limit and focus the work of any office or individual.

12. *Anglo-American Cataloging Rules*, 2nd ed. (Chicago: ALA, 1978).

Chapter 3

Anatomy of a Markup Language

If you have an understanding of how markup languages work, you will appreciate more fully the importance of some of the details we are covering. This chapter will explain the basics of markup languages and therefore of EAD itself. As you read it, strive to develop a general understanding of markup and EAD. Do not scare yourself by thinking that you must absorb all the details in the text below. Strive for an image of how markup works.

Format vs. Function

When we sit down to write a business letter, we do several things without usually appreciating their complexity and importance. For instance, we start by entering our own address and the date on which we are writing the letter. If we use letterhead stationary, we know that the return address appears on the paper already and we simply add the date. Next, we insert the name and address of the person who will receive the letter. We follow that information with a greeting, and follow it with the body of the letter. The body of the letter may contain a single sentence, or it may go on for several pages. Regardless, at the end we include a kind closing thought and sign our name.

As you read the preceding paragraph, you probably developed a mental image of the letter and could "see" the features as they received mention in the description, even though the narrative itself gives no indication of where the elements of the letter might appear in relation to each other. Somewhere in your education, someone taught you how to format a business letter.

We have become so accustomed to the look of a business letter that we do not consciously distinguish between the structure or format (i.e., the placement of its various elements) and the function (i.e., the informational value each element provides). We have absorbed our awareness of data element, data structure, data value, and data format completely unconsciously, but we understand them.

In markup languages, the distinction between the look of the document and its informational value matters. A business letter carries two addresses—the sender's and the receiver's. Each address would convey its information regardless of where it appeared on the page, but because we have standardized the format of the letter, where the address appears on the page helps us distinguish between the sender of the letter and its recipient.

Our paper-based society developed a standard format for writing business letters centuries ago, thus allowing writers to concentrate on providing effective content instead of fussing over how the letter should look. We have absorbed the formula so fully that we find it hard to consider sending or receiving a business letter formatted any other way. But we *could* format it another way. The format does not alter the content; it only alters the speed with which we both create and read the letter as a business letter.

And so it is with all common documents. When we sit down to write on paper, we mentally format the document—a memo or a letter or a poem or a recipe—before we start writing. We visualize it on the page, so to speak, and then place the elements according to our vision. Once we hae the work on the paper, we cannot easily change it; the format and the content have merged on the surface of the page and will remain that way until the paper no longer exists.

Regardless of the scale—a single-sheet handwritten note or an international newspaper—paper-based publication works the same way. Electronic publication works differently. Computers do not visualize where we want them to put information. Modern word processors have in them a number of programs that allow us to think the computer "knows" how we want our documents to look—but that is an illusion. Remember: a computer is as dumb as a hubbard squash.[1] It needs instructions to do anything.

Further, electronic documents on a computer screen do not have a permanent existence. They come and go at the click of a button. Since the medium that produces them gives them no permanence, electronic documents typically carry within them the "programming" that distinguishes between the information's function and its format. We do not usually see that programming, but no computer document appears on the screen without it.

The fact that computers need instruction to do anything, and the fact that they create impermanent images, allows us to make use of the distinction between function and format in a way that paper does not. The distinction creates the potential for great flexibility in the way we present information electronically.

XML

An electronic publishing environment called Extensible Markup Language (XML) establishes the rules which underlie EAD.[2] As you read, concentrate on getting a mental image of the system at work—do not worry about how and why.

XML relies on two components to define the function of a piece of text: elements (also called tags) and attributes.

Elements

EAD consists of a set of about 145 *elements* that describe the functions of various portions of a finding aid—elements such as <title>, <scopecontent>, <bioghist>, <container>, etc. encase the portions of information that serve that function. The fact that the tag name exists within angled brackets allows the computer, and us, to distinguish between markup tags and the content of the document. The opening tag, <element>, indicates where the element starts, and the closing tag, </element>, indicates where it stops. Both the computer and the human understand that text within angled brackets represents some sort of description of the text it surrounds. The computer sees the tag as a command which carries limitations and requirements governing its use in relation to others. Programs called XML editors usually have a feature which alerts you, the user, to the limitations and requirements applied to the tags.

Attributes

Declaring the function of a piece of text with an element may not provide enough information about it. For example, archivists house materials in many types of containers such as boxes, folders, map drawers, etc. The developers of the EAD tag set could have included a tag for each, but to avoid creating an unmanageably large set of tags, they used a device called an "attribute." We can modify generic tags, like <container>, if we insert an *attribute* and its value into the tag. EAD calls the attribute for distinguishing container types *type*. We can define our containers as <container type="box"> and <container type="folder"> to clarify our description.

Using a combination of elements and attributes, we can create remarkably exact descriptions of the text in our documents. We can then use those descriptions to help researchers pinpoint the information they seek. In the tagging of the example on the next page, note the use of attributes to clarify and standardize potentially confusing data, such as dates and names.

Stylesheets

Robust markup languages define the function of text.[3] For instance, every archival series and subseries has a title. If we tag the title of the series and subseries (component levels one and two, or c01 and c02) of the electronic inventory of the Fictitious College Records as <unittitle>s and we tag the dates as <unitdate>s, those tags, defining the function of those words, will remain forever. We can then, depending on our needs, ask the computer to format each tag in many different ways. Using another program called a stylesheet, we can have the computer format the series titles, the <c01>s, and the subseries titles, the <c02>s, using any font we choose, rendered in any color we fancy. Further, by using the same stylesheet for all our inventories, we can create an absolutely consistent presentation of our holdings of two dozen or two thousand finding aids. And when we tire of BOLD SMALL CAP titles on our computer screens, we can change them all to *Bold Italics* by making a single change in the stylesheet. We do not need to touch the inventories themselves. For example, an inventory marked up in EAD might look like this:

```
<c01 level="series">
   <unittitle>Office of the President,</unittitle>
   <unitdate normal="1889–07/1942-09" >June 1889–September 1942
   </unitdate>
   <c02 level="subseries">
      <unittitle>Administration of Fearless L. Fictitious,</unittitle>
      <unitdate normal="1889-07/1929-06"> July 1889– June 1929
      </unitdate> </c02>
    <c02>
      <unittitle level="subseries">Administration
      of Cornelius J. Fictitious, </unittitle>
      <unitdate normal="1929-07/1942-02"> July 1929– February
      1942</unitdate></c02>
</c01>
<c01 level="series">
   <unittitle>Office of the Dean of Students,
   </unittitle>
   <unitdate> 1889–1942</unitdate>
</c01>
```

Having defined the function of the text with the markup, we can now tell the computer how to format it. We may want to highlight certain aspects, so, for example, we could tell the computer to display all of the text tagged

<c01> as italic, and to add other features to other parts of the same tag. We want to show that the <c02> components nest within the <c01> components, so we ask for indentation. In the Cascading Style Sheet (CSS2) language,[4] the commands would look like this:

---

c01 {font-style: italic}

c02 {font-style: normal; text-indent: 8cm}

unitdate {text-decoration: underline}

On the screen, all the text coded within the <c01> and <c02> tags would appear in the font-style assigned to that whole tag. In addition, the text in the <unitdate> tags, will have an underline in response to the specific command for that tag, regardless where it appears. On the screen, the text would appear as follows:

Office of the President, <u>June 1889–September 1942</u>

   Administration of Fearless L. Fictitious, <u>July 1889–June 1929</u>

   Administration of Cornelius J. Fictitious, <u>July 1929–February 1942</u>

Office of the Dean of Students, <u>1889–1942</u>

EAD encourages clearly defined data elements to support the computer's ability to work with the markup. XML allows you to create stylesheets as separate but complementary programs. The more consistently and precisely you have defined your data, the more easily will the computer display it uniformly. Clearly and uniformly defined data elements also support search engine functioning—a topic that will arise in chapter 6.

Structure of EAD

EAD supports the principles of a hierarchical structure within the collection as discussed in chapter 2. The whole document falls within the opening <ead>

tag and its partner at the very end, the closing </ead> tag. Between those two tags, EAD has three discrete parts tagged: <eadheader>, <frontmatter>, and <archdesc>.

The <eadheader> section holds information about the electronic finding aid and has value only in an electronic environment. You need not use it or even think about it when you create a paper finding aid.

The <frontmatter> section holds information useful for the creation of a title page for the web-published inventory. <Frontmatter> reuses information you collect and organize in other places, so, again, you need not use it or even think about it when you create a paper finding aid.

The actual description of the archival materials and associated administrative and contextual information appears in a section called <archdesc>, "archival description." It holds more information than any other section of the inventory.

That is EAD's main structure. The three "wrapper" tags—tags which touch only other tags, not any actual data itself—fit within the "wrapper" of the root <ead> tag but do not intersect with each other; they appear one after the other as illustrated below.

```
<ead>
   <eadheader> Tags and data </eadheader>
   <frontmatter> Tags and data </frontmatter>
   <archdesc> Tags and data </archdesc>
</ead>
```

EAD allows a bewildering amount of flexibility for structuring the markup of an inventory. Regional and state consortia have developed guidelines outlining what they regard as best practices for EAD markup. You can easily find good reasons to follow them, even though you plan to work on paper. Notice, however, that their completeness and supporting documentation vary widely.

The Research Libraries Group[5] (RLG) has, for a number of years, actively sought to pull together the inventories of historical repositories to create a national union database of archival resources.[6] They also have developed a format that data should meet for successful inclusion in their database. They have published the format as the *Best Practice Guidelines*.[7] RLG has refined the model they use so that now it represents an extremely workable design for a wide variety of inventories from a wide variety of repositories. You could adopt those guidelines instead of a more local set. You should get to know your options fairly well before you choose a guide to follow. Given that RLG casts the widest net, this book includes it to demonstrate how best practice guidelines work.

Within the <archdesc> tag, RLG asks for the following information and recommends the following order.[8] Notice how easily you can "read" the tags and understand them.

<origination> with one of the four name choices: <persname |
    corpname | famname | name> the name of the creator,
<unittitle> the name of the collection,
<unitdate> the span of dates covered by the collection,
<physdesc> a description of the count, dimensions, etc., of the materi-
    als,
<phystech> description of physical conditions or circumstances that
    affect how the collection should be stored or used,
a very brief summary statement about the materials, their
    creator, and the circumstances of their creation,
<originalsloc> information about the originals if the collection in hand
    is a copy,
<repository> name and contact information of the repository holding
    the collection,
<unitid> a unique identifier for the collection,
<langmaterial> the language(s) of the material of the collection,

---

<bioghist> personal biographical information or agency history of the creator of the collection,

<scopecontent> a description of the scope and content of the collection,

<arrangement> how the collection has been arranged,

<fileplan> information about any classification scheme used for managing the collection when in the hands of the creator,

<controlaccess> controlled access terms for the contents of the collection, such as standardized versions of proper nouns in the collection, or subject headings,

<accessrestrict> any restrictions on access,

<accruals> quantity or frequency of anticipated accruals,

<acqinfo> information on the original acquisition of the collection,

<altformavail> information on alternative forms of materials in the collection, such as microfilm versions,

<appraisal> information about the appraisal of the collection and any disposition decisions relating to it,

<custodhist> the provenance of the collection (i.e., its custodial history),

<prefercite> the preferred citation for the collection,

<processinfo> information about the processing of the collection,

<userestrict> any restrictions on the uses of the collection,

<relatedmaterial> listing of other materials that relate to the collection in some significant way,

<separatedmaterial> a listing of any materials that arrived with the collection but have been separated from it,

<otherfindaid> information about addition finding aids to all or part of this collection,

information about any published or produced work about or involving the use of the materials,

<note> miscellaneous notes and descriptive information,

<odd> other descriptive data which does not fit into any other category.

Most of these <archdesc> tags call for a paragraph or more of prose explanation; most do not require extensive codes or standardized language. They invite you to tell the story of the collection, its history, and the decisions that you have made about it.

Description of Subordinate Components, <dsc>

After <archdesc> has pulled together all this information about the whole collection, it provides a description of component parts in a section called Description of Subordinate Components, tagged <dsc>.

Typically subordinate components consist of series (and subseries, etc.) and their container lists. Since the subordinate components define the hierarchical structure of the inventory, each starts with a wrapper that defines its level in the hierarchy. Although the computer does not need to have these levels spelled out, humans do, so EAD provides tags which number the layers to the depth of <c12>. It also provides an unnumbered <c> tag which can go infinitely deep.

The highest component, a series, gets tagged Component Level 1, <c01>. A subseries of that series would have the tag Component Level 2, <c02>. The next level, perhaps some file folders that hold the documents, would have the tag showing their place in the hierarchy as Component Level 3, <c03>. Finally, if a particular document warrants highlighting, it would become Component Level 4, <c04>.[9]

Look at how Sue Ann Fictitious's component of the Fictitious Family Papers would break down for EAD.[10]

<ead>
<eadheader> Tags and data </eadheader>
<frontmatter>An Electronic Inventory of the Fictitious Family Papers, 1850–1999</frontmatter>
<archdesc>Tags and data
<dsc><head>Container List</head>

```
<c01>Sue Ann Fictitious Papers, 1961–1999
    <c02>Education, 1965–1988
        <c03>Fictitious College, 1961–1965</c03>
        <c03>Rainy University, 1969–1970</c03>
        <c03>Snowy University, 1979–1985
            <c04>Papers, 1979–1980
                <c05>Thesis, 1980–1986
                    <c06>Manuscript notes, 1979–1983</c06>
                    <c06>Monograph notes, 1980–1983</c06>
                    <c06>Newspaper notes, 1978–1983</c06>
                    <c06>Oral history notes, 1980–1983</c06>
                    <c06>Drafts, 1983–1986
                        <c07>Final draft, 1986</c07>
                    </c06>
                </c05>
            </c04>
        </c03>
        <c03>Smokey University, 1983–1988</c03>
    </c02>
    <c02>Careers</c02>
  </c01>
</dsc>
</archdesc>
</ead>
```

Notice that the number of the component tag indicates its depth into the hierarchy—and nothing more. It does not represent a chronological or numerical ordering of any sort. From one inventory to another, various component parts will not have the same hierarchical level—an item level in another collection might have <c04> rather than the <c07> it has here. That's fine.

Notice also that each component eventually closes, but only after all its own subordinate components close—again, like nested Russian dolls.

As the example shows, subordinate components of a collection may have an extensive and complicated structure and history. For that reason, DACS and ISAD(G)v2 encourage the collection of data about subordinate components, and EAD encodes it. While both standards work on the principle that information applied at a higher level (e.g., the collection level) applies to all levels below unless otherwise specified, both allow—and encourage—the addition of information where it differs from the inherited information.

For example, if the bulk of the Fictitious family papers came from Eleanora Fictitious, Sue Ann's mother, but Sue Ann donated her own papers, you would want to include the <acqinfo> for this series at the series level. Sue Ann has decided that she wants to close the notes from the oral histories she took while researching her thesis. You should indicate this in an <accessrestrict> note at the <c01> level, explaining that all materials, with the exception of the oral history notes, are open to the public. At the <c06> level you would include a fuller explanation with details about how long the restriction holds and who, if anyone, has the authority to override it. While you will have done a general <bioghist> note on the Fictitious family which includes Sue Ann, you would put a fuller <bioghist> for Sue Ann at this level.

<c01>Sue Ann Fictitious Papers, 1961–1999
  <acqinfo> Explanation</acqinfo>
  <accessrestrict>Statement about use of Ms. Fictitious's materials, referencing restrictions on the oral history notes</accessrestrict>
  <bioghist>About Sue Ann </bioghist>
  <scopecontent> About her papers</scopecontent>
  <c02>Education, 1965–1988

     ...

    <c05>Thesis, 1980–1986

```
            <c06>Manuscript notes, 1979–1983</c06>
            <c06>Monograph notes, 1980–1983</c06>
            <c06>Newspaper notes, 1978–1983</c06>
            <c06>Oral history notes, 1980–1983
                  <accessrestrict>Full explanation of the
                        restrictions imposed.
                  </accessrestrict>
            </c06>
            <c06>Drafts, 1983–1986
                  <c07>Final draft, 1986</c07>
            </c06>
      </c05>
            …
   </c02>
</c01>
```

All the data elements that apply at the collection level can also apply at all component levels, except one. For fairly obvious reasons you will not need to use the repository name and location at the series level. All others apply to a lower level if circumstances warrant; it goes almost without saying that EAD will accommodate them.

Notes

1. An observation first made to me by David M. Dow in Hardwick, Vermont, in 1981. It was true then and it remains true today.

2. Actually Daniel Pitti developed the original version of EAD in SGML, an earlier, more difficult markup language standard. The EADWG converted EAD to XML between 2001and 2003.

3. Markup languages, like cheeses, range in strength. Many small, special-purpose languages exist which have limited capacity and may even have the stylesheet function built into the tag set.

4. CSS provides a clear command structure for demonstrating the points here, but it is only one of many stylesheet languages.

5. www.rlg.org.

6. www.rlg.org/arr/index.html and www.rlg.org/primary/index.html.

7. www.rlg.org/rlgead/eadguides.html.

8. See chapter 4 for a fuller explanation of each element.

9. EAD also allows the tagging of various component levels using an unnumbered component tag, <c>. While computers find them easy to keep track of, humans do not. But if you have a collection that goes deeper than twelve component levels, EAD can handle it with <c>.

10. Here tagging is limited to those elements which address the topic of the text. *This example does not illustrate full EAD markup.*

Chapter 4

Getting Organized and Collecting Information

Consider the typical inventory. Although repositories have developed a wide variety of idiosyncratic approaches for their inventories, the final documents usually contain a fundamental set of elements presented in a fairly predictable way.[1] The documents start with facts about the repository and the collection. They then provide a statement of the scope and contents of the collection, the history of the collection, and some biographical or historical information about the creators of the collection. Having created the larger picture, they describe in greater detail the series that make up the collection. This "greater detail" includes information similar to that provided for the whole collection, but tailored to the series. Finally they present a container list, describing in some detail the contents of the collection, typically one folder or item at a time. In the end, the inventory defines a hierarchy of information displaying the content of the collection and the way various parts relate to other parts.

Obviously you can think of lots of variations on the theme above. For instance, some collections include a lot of nonpaper items and therefore may include many item-level descriptions of photographs, maps, published volumes, audiotapes, etc. Other collections, usually small ones, have only one series. Still other collections exist because a collector or the archivist compiled them from a variety of disparate sources or accessions. There is no question that variations exist. But, as a general rule, the description above portrays with essential accuracy the vast majority of finding aids.

Description of historical collections depends on hierarchical description. In their container lists, historical collections usually contain a variety of series within series within other series. Archivists have learned to show that one series describes part of a larger series. The nesting of such series may go many layers deep and end up looking like a detailed outline.[2]

Therefore, think about describing your collections in terms of levels of description. Higher levels describe the whole body of material and help patrons get a sense of the collection as a whole. Middle level information describes series or other components; it gives the researcher an overview of the parts of the collection. Lower level information provides details inappropriate at higher levels, describing folders or individual items. You may quite legitimately *mention* general characteristics of various lower component parts while describing at higher levels, avoiding details until you reach a lower component level.

This chapter focuses on what you need to have on hand to create EAD-compliant finding aids on paper and what information you will need to collect. Once collected, the information will fit into a format that can serve as a standard repository-wide introduction to your collections.

Getting Organized

EAD encoding is a labor intensive enterprise under the best of circumstances, and as we all know, labor costs more than anything. Looking to the day when your repository may have an opportunity to convert its paper inventories to EAD-encoded inventories, you can assure yourself and your successors the least expensive conversion possible by already having all the information DACS, ISAD(G)v2, and EAD call for in the inventories you have created. Further, you can reduce the cost of the labor you expend accumulating that information by organizing the collecting of crucial information into a finely tuned routine which everyone in the repository understands and follows. So here we stop to look at your information-gathering system.

All repositories do essentially the same work: they appraise, acquire, arrange, describe, preserve, and provide access to historical materials. Each function has two aspects: the actual labor of the task itself, and the documentation of the task. Every repository organizes its labor and record keeping to suit itself, and within each institution the process has, no doubt, changed over time in response to new philosophies, personnel, and information technologies. In particular the documentation of various activities in relation to your holdings may vary widely in both form and format over the years. This variety introduces the probability of both inefficiency and redundancy at any given time and incoherence across time. But perhaps not; perhaps your system works perfectly.

The perfect system has a highly structured way of collecting and storing the information the repository needs to meet its legal, fiscal, ethical, and political responsibilities toward its donors, users, institution, and holdings. It has forms which collect all pertinent data in standard formats and it stores all the information in one or two places. It has models or templates for staff to follow if they must create a document on a blank sheet of paper. In the perfect system, all who have responsibility for collecting or recording data receive thorough training in the completion or creation of data forms they must use, however infrequently. Each form, like those mentioned above, comes with clear directions to refresh the memory of infrequent users.

Recognizing that good forms help create the accumulation of good and complete data, ARMA International and the Society of American Archivists jointly published a book of generic forms for historical repositories to use.[3] The publishers grant the purchaser of each book explicit permission to reproduce the forms it contains. The book even includes a CD which holds electronic versions of each form so repositories can alter them to suit their purposes more precisely.

The SAA/ARMA book recognizes that data collection happens over the life cycle of an archival accession as it moves through the administrative and technical processing procedures in the institution that holds it. The forms provide reminders to include certain information elements; they also provide a generic but uniform structure to hold it.

The perfect system also includes a full collection of reference materials that provide basic background information about all the areas of your collecting interests, starting with a few predictable types of reference materials.

You will need at least a good encyclopedia for general knowledge, and probably a couple more specialized encyclopedias to support your major collecting areas.

Similarly, you will need several types of dictionaries. You will need a general dictionary, of course, but also sources of insight into the meaning of terms in their historical context. You may also need discipline-specific dictionaries for your collecting areas.

You will need biographical sources of many varieties. Collected biographies and biographical directories will provide basic facts about a wide range of people, whereas more focused biographies provide more information on fewer people. Biographies of local notables usually prove hardest to find, which causes archivists to acquire and use sources which may not qualify as "good" examples of the biographer's art. They may be poorly written, poorly organized, poorly bound, and may interpret all persons mentioned as models of virtue. Regardless, if they provide fundamental facts about the life, education, marriage, etc. of local notables, archivists will use them and be grateful for them.

Ditto for local histories, especially histories of local institutions and communities. You may recognize that the story is flawed and the interpretation weak, but if the facts are accurate, you will want to acquire and use the work—it may be the only one available.

You will also want a core collection of what librarians call "ready reference" materials—books chock-full of facts of a wide-ranging nature. What day of the week was July 8, 1776? How many Swedes immigrated to the United States in 1887? Who won the Nobel Peace Prize in 1947? How high is Mt. Tom? Almanacs both general and local, handbooks, directories, compendiums of historical statistics, and the like provide this kind of factual data without a lot of textual interpretation. Their format makes them very quick to use.

Develop a collection of bibliographies and indexes for areas that relate to your collection. If you need information not contained in any of your other works, a good bibliography can suggest other sources. Indexes and bibliographies of local interest will prove especially valuable but may be hard to find.

You'll need geographical sources, as well. Maps, gazetteers, and atlases, both current and historical, will provide information on name changes, economic changes, and infrastructure changes of all sorts.

Collect documents issued by governments and nongovernmental organizations at all levels. Both special and annual reports contain statistics, proposals, research reports, and white papers. You may find myriad forms of information in them to provide background and context for your collections.

Finally, you have your own work to turn to. Among your various finding aids you will find information derived from earlier collections which may contextualize later materials.

Without an extensive collection of reference materials, you will find yourself wanting to provide contextual information that you do not have. Because the reference materials you need will focus more on historical data than current data, once you have them, you will use them for years into the future. Do not hesitate; when a new source comes on the market that fills your information needs, acquire it.

The perfect archives descriptive system also makes all published standards readily available to the staff. You cannot overdo your adherence to standards—standards for data content and format. Two complementary pieces of research, both presented at the Society of American Archivists Annual Meeting in 2002 and subsequently published in the *Journal of Archival Organization*, detail the problems that arise when repositories do not adopt and adhere to standards.[4]

If you want to create standardized inventories, you must understand what standards to use, when to use them, and how to use them. Further, you must have them readily at hand. "Readily at hand" may mean a bookcase of published documents; it may mean a number of computer-based databases on an in-house computer; it may mean an in-house Web page linking to Internet sources; it probably means a combination of the above. Regardless of how you provide the resources, staff who need to know the standard name, wording, or format for any given bit of information should know where to find the standard that addresses it and how to use the tool that provides it.[5]

One of the standards tools you may find your institution needs most—an authority file of local names—probably will not come from an outside institution; you probably will need to create it yourself. All repositories typically contain wonderful materials by individuals and groups unknown outside the local area or outside their field of expertise. When describing those materials in your repository, you will have to create a record, called an "authority record," which documents the "authorized" name you have chosen, the source from which you derived it, and variations that it should replace. You will find much more on this issue in chapter 6.

The perfect system does not magically appear one afternoon. It grows out of a thorough understanding of your institutional needs, a wide variety of standards, and the generally accepted best practices. Dennis Meissner described how the Minnesota Historical Society reassessed its finding aids in light of EAD; his article describes their self-study and suggests a way to go about the process.[6] As a result of their self-study, the MHS has redesigned the way they organize their inventories and the way they go about creating them. Clay Redding makes a compelling argument that everyone should rethink and redesign their finding aids with EAD in mind.[7] Of course, no EAD police will pound on your door if you don't, but if you are serious about EAD compliance, you should think seriously about reexamining the way you do your finding aids.

Now that you have a sense of the information you will need to organize, and you have an idea of where to get forms to guide you, consider what you will need to incorporate into your new system to support the information gathering process.

ISAD(G)v2 calls for twenty-six specific data elements, all easily collected on one or more fact-sheets as the collection moves through the acquisition, arrangement, and description processes. DACS calls for twenty-five. EAD provides tagging for a number of other data elements either not differentiated by or not included in DACS or ISAD(G)v2. For example, EAD has two tags, <relatedmaterial> and <seperatedmaterial>, which ISAD(G)v2 and DACS conceptually lump together. Another example: DACS calls for the name of your repository, which ISAD(G)v2 does not, but which EAD provides a <repository> tag for. Yet another: EAD provides a tag for an , which ISAD(G)v2 and DACS do not object to; neither requests it, however. As you see, the incongruence between the two standards does not reflect any genuine conflict. But clearly you could wind up with a major headache as you sort all this out.

However, if you adopt the RLG *Best Practice Guidelines* to guide your markup choices, you will automatically meet the requirements for both DACS and ISAD(G)v2, without consciously thinking about the differences between DACS and ISAD(G)v2 and how it all works in EAD.[8]

Key Data Elements

Below you will find a list of data elements you will want to collect to provide everything DACS, ISAD(G)v2, and the RLG's *Best Practice Guidelines* want to know from and about the collection. The text presents each element by name, followed by the ISAD(G)v2 rule number. ISAD(G)v2 labels only six as essential. All essential ISAD(G) elements have the phrase "Considered essential by ISAD(G)v2" in the text that follows them.

After each ISAD(G)v2 element, you will find the DACS rule that correlates to it. DACS varies the minimum (essential) data element set according to whether the record represents single-level or multilevel description. All DACS' minimum elements have the phrase "DACS minimum for level description" in the text that follows them.

Following the DACS element name, you will find the EAD tag(s) that represent the element in a marked-up document.

Following the EAD coding, you will find a code which indicates the status of the data element in the RLG *Best Practice Guidelines*. In the guidelines,

RLG describes the level of importance it puts on the various content elements. Anything that either EAD or the RLG requires appears as RLG: M (mandatory). When a mandatory data element may not exist in every collection, RLG uses MA for "mandatory if available," listed here as RLG: MA. Elements which RLG sees as useful but not essential it codes as R for "recommended." They appear here as RLG: R. Finally, RLG recognizes that some elements add to the description but labels them as O for "optional"; here noted as RLG: O.

Finally, you will find a description of the element and an example as it appears in a finding aid. For examples of the actual application of the tags in a marked-up document, see DACS or the *Encoded Archival Description Tag Library.*[9]

You will notice as you compare the three sets of "rules" about data elements that all three sets basically agree on what constitutes essential information and what is just good to have. EAD can handle all elements listed.

Unique Identifier [ISAD(G)v2] or Reference Code [DACS]

Considered essential by ISAD(G)v2. ISAD(G)v2 rule: 3.1.1.
DACS minimum for single-level and multilevel description. DACS element: 2.1.
EAD element: <eadid> and <unitid>
RLG: M.

This element serves to differentiate one collection from all other collections in the world—literally. DACS calls for a local repository Reference Code for all materials described within a repository and endorses the ISAD(G)v2 formula for those which will have descriptive records made available outside the repository. The ISAD(G)v2 formula for creating such a code calls for:

1. A country code from the latest version of ISO 3166-1: *Codes for the Representation of Names of Countries*: www.iso.ch/iso/en/ prods_services/iso3166ma/02iso_3166_code_lists/list_en1.html.

2. A repository code from your national repository code standard or other unique location identifier. The Library of Congress and the National Library of Canada assign repository codes and maintain the list of assigned codes in their respective countries. These repository codes are constructed in accordance with the latest version of ISO 15511 (*International standard identifier for libraries and related organizations*). The Library of Congress database, available on the Web, contains codes for larger Canadian repositories: www.loc.gov/marc/organizations/orgshome.html.

3. A specific local reference code, accession number, control number, or other unique identifier. Your repository must, of course, take responsibility for its own internal system of collection codes.

The combination of national, repository, and collection identifier assures that no other collection in the world will have the exact same code.

University of Kentucky Manuscripts Archives:
  Harriette Simpson Arnow Papers, 1927–1967 (us-kyu-1M81M2)

New Mexico State Records Center and Archives:
  Inventory of the Spanish Archives of New Mexico I, 1685–1912
  Collection number: (us-nmar-1972-002)

Name and Location of Repository

DACS minimum for single-level and multilevel description. DACS element: 2.2.
EAD element: <repository>
RLG: M.

This element identifies the repository that holds the materials referenced in the record. It should include location and other contact information. ISAD(G)v2 does not call for a comparable element.

Title by Which the Collection Will Be Known

Considered essential by ISAD(G)v2 at all component levels. ISAD(G)v2 rule: 3.1.2.
DACS minimum for single-level and multilevel description. DACS element: 2.3.
EAD element: <unittitle>
RLG: M.

Unlike book catalogers who take the "official" title from the title page, archivists usually create titles for their collections. Traditionally the titles of collections, series, folders, etc. consist of the name of the creator(s) and a word or phrase which describes the contents. If the unit holds one or two types of materials, the title is based on the form of material.

Henry Sheldon Museum of Vermont History, Middlebury, Vt.:
   James Family Diaries and Accounts
   Phineas Spaulding Ledger and Daybook
   Boardman Family Letters

If a collection holds more than two types of materials, use a collective term. While Canadians use *fonds* to refer to both personal and corporate materials, archivists in the United States make a distinction between private (individual or family) *papers* and corporate *records*. The term *collection* as part of a title usually refers to a collection consciously brought together by a collector.

Henry Sheldon Museum of Vermont History, Middlebury, Vt.:
   Lucius Shaw Papers
   Rutland and Burlington Railroad Records

Louisiana and Lower Mississippi Valley Collections, LSU Libraries:
   Hispanic American Collection (a collection of materials relating to
   Hispanic America)

Occasionally materials have a formal title supplied by the creator or former owner. If a formal title exists, use it, unless evidence within the collection casts doubt on the accuracy of the formal title. In that case, supply a title.

Henry Sheldon Museum of Vermont History, Middlebury, Vt.:
Park Hotel Register (name embossed on the spine of the volume)
"Scrapbook 087: O.B. Clarke's Forgeries, 1863" (name written on the front of a scrapbook created by Henry Sheldon)

Special Collections, Bailey/Howe Library, University of Vermont:
"From Down to the Village" (mss. of a book of poems by David Budbill)

Apply to the component level the same method for creating the collection title.

Louisiana and Lower Mississippi Valley Collections, LSU Libraries:
Andry (Michel Thomassin) and Family Papers, 1840–1882 (bulk, 1858–1879)
Series II. Legal Documents, 1840–1870

Dates Included in the Collection

Considered essential by ISAD(G)v2. ISAD(G)v2 rule: 3.1.3.
DACS minimum for single-level and multilevel description. DACS element: 2.4.
EAD element: <unitdate>
RLG: M.

The collection date should reflect the creation, accumulation, and/or maintenance and use of the materials in the collection. Historical records usually teem with dates. The ISAD(G)v2 and DACS date elements ask for the dates which reflect the actual creation of the materials, which may not reflect the dates referred to in the content. A letter written in the 1990s, for example, might discuss events from the 1970s. The dates of the events discussed belong in the Scope and Content notes.

Special Collections, Bailey/Howe Library, University of Vermont:
  East Charlotte Baptist Church Records, 1882–1943

Louisiana and Lower Mississippi Valley Collections LSU Libraries:
  Andry (Michel Thomassin) and Family Papers, 1840–1882 (bulk, 1858–1879)
  Series II. Legal Documents, 1840–1870

Level of Description

Considered essential by ISAD(G)v2. ISAD(G)v2 rule: 3.1.4.
DACS minimum for single level and multilevel description. DACS element: 3.1.
EAD element: LEVEL attribute in <archdesc> and <c> or <c1> to <c12> elements.
RLG: M.

Understanding the level of description takes on a rather intuitive quality on a paper document, as the indentation indicates the level of description. In an electronic environment, however, that level may become less obvious. EAD has a required attribute in the <archdesc> element for the LEVEL of the description and an optional LEVEL attribute in all the numbered <c#> and unnumbered <c> component elements. For easy coding, define the levels in the paper document.

Special Collections, Bailey/Howe Library, University of Vermont:
  East Charlotte Baptist Church Records, 1882–1943

> Louisiana and Lower Mississippi Valley Collections, LSU Libraries:
>   Andry (Michel Thomassin) and Family Papers, 1840–1882 (bulk,
>   1858–1879)
> Series II. Legal Documents, 1840–1870

Physical Description of the Collection [ISAD(G)v2] or Extent [DACS]

Considered essential by ISAD(G)v2. ISAD(G)v2 rule: 3.1.5.
DACS minimum for single-level and multilevel description. DACS element: 2.5.
EAD element: <physdesc> with <extent>, <dimensions>, <genreform>, and
<physfacet>.
RLG: M.

Given the range of materials that may reside in a repository, the physical descriptions will vary widely in their details, but the principles will remain consistent. We can categorize materials into the following large groupings: textual materials, photographs and other graphic materials, maps and other cartographic materials, architectural and technical drawings, moving images, sound recordings, and records (graphic images or textual materials) in electronic form. The physical description should include information about the extent of the collection, characteristics of the materials, including any technical requirements needed to use them, and dimensions of the materials and/or their containers. The amount of detail you provide will vary depending on the characteristics of the collection under discussion and your repository's policies. A full description also serves an administrative function in that it provides a record of the amount of space, type of storage units, etc., needed to store all or part of the collection.

As always, choosing specific designations from a standard vocabulary will assure your records' compatibility with the records of other repositories. See the following sources for terms identifying specific classes of:

1. Textual material

> Peterson, Toni, dir. *Art and Architecture Thesaurus,* 2nd ed. New York: Oxford University Press on behalf of the J. Paul Getty Trust, 1994; or online at www.getty.edu/research/tools/vocabulary/aat/.

2. Architectural material

> Peterson, Toni, dir. *Art and Architecture Thesaurus,* 2nd ed. New York: Oxford University Press on behalf of the Paul Getty Trust, 1994; or online at www.getty.edu/research/tools/vocabulary/aat/.

> Porter, Vicki, and Thornes, Robin. *A Guide to the Description of Architectural Drawings.* New York: Published on behalf of the Getty Art History Information Program [by] G.K. Hall, c1994.

3. Graphic material

> Peterson, Toni, dir. *Art and Architecture Thesaurus,* 2nd ed. New York: Oxford University Press on behalf of the J. Paul Getty Trust, 1994; or online at www.getty.edu/research/tools/vocabulary/aat/.

> *Thesaurus for Graphic Materials.* Washington, D.C.: Library of Congress, 1995; or online at www.loc.gov/rr/print/tgm1/ and lcweb.loc.gov/rr/print/tgm2/.

See the following sources for specific material designations for the description of:

1. Cartographic materials, particularly at the item level

> *Cartographic Materials: A Manual of Interpretation for AACR2.* Hugo Stibbe, Vivien Cartmell, and Velma Parker, editors. Ottawa: Canadian Library Association, 1982.

2. Moving image materials, particularly at the item level

> *The FIAF Cataloguing Rules for Film Archives.* Munich: K.G. Saur, 1991.

> White-Hensen, Wendy. *Archival Moving Image Materials: A Cataloging Manual,* 2nd ed. Washington, D.C.: Library of Congress, 2000.

> *The IASA Cataloguing Rules: A Manual for the Description of Sound Recordings and Related Audiovisual Media.* Stockholm: International Association of Sound and Audiovisual Archives, 1999; or online at www.llgc.org.uk/iasa/icat/icat001.htm.

3. Sound recordings, particularly at the item level

> *The IASA Cataloguing Rules: A Manual for the Description of Sound Recordings and Related Audiovisual Media.* Stockholm: International Association of Sound and Audiovisual Archives, 1999; or online at www.llgc.org.uk/iasa/icat/icat001.htm.

Person, Family, or Corporate Body Responsible for Creating the Collection

Considered essential by ISAD(G)v2. ISAD(G)v2 rule: 3.2.1.
DACS minimum for single-level and multilevel description. DACS element: 2.6.
EAD element: <origination> with <persname>, <famname>, or <corpname>.
RLG: M.

Generally this means including as part of the title of the collection the name of the creator or collector predominantly responsible for the existence of the collection. Typically you will use the natural order of the name by which the creator is generally known, written in the language of the collection. While this sounds straightforward enough, you will undoubtedly run into problem situations, for example, lots of "creators" in a collection making the task of determining the "predominant" party difficult, corporate bodies whose names have changed, collections which clearly belong together but have no evidence of their origins, and collections which have no true creator. While DACS includes "Name of Creators" as Identity Element 2.6, in a later chapter it provides extensive directions on identifying creators. DACS also gives extensive directions for formatting names of creators in chapters 12 and 14. More guidance in the choice and formatting of names appear in the manuals below.

> Joint Steering Committee of AACR. *Anglo-American Cataloging Rules.* Ottawa: Canadian Library Association, 2002.—AACR2, the library standard in the English-speaking world.

> Bureau of Canadian Archivists. *Rules for Archival Description.* Ottawa: The Bureau, 1990–1900s.—RAD, the Canadian standard.

Proctor, Margaret, and Cook, Michael. *Manual of Archival Description,* 3rd. ed. Burlington, Vt.: Gower, 2000.—MAD, the British standard.

Hensen, Steven L. *Archives, Personal Papers, and Manuscripts: A Cataloging Manual for Archival Repositories, Historical Societies, and Manuscript Libraries.* Chicago: Society of American Archivists, 1989.— APPM, formerly the standard American manual.

Biographical or Historical Information [ISAD(G)v2] or Administrative/ Biographical History [DACS]

ISAD(G)v2 rule: 3.2.2.
DACS element: 2.7.
EAD element: <bioghist>
RLG: M.

The administrative/biographical historical notes provide historical information about the institutional unit or individuals responsible for creating, accumulating, or maintaining the materials. This information provides the historical context out of which the materials grew. When primary responsibility for the creation of a collection involves more than one institution or person, you will want to create separate biographical/historical notes for each.

When describing individuals or families, the biographical notes should provide information that casts light on the life, activities, and relationships of the individuals and/or families involved. Where you can, include summaries including name(s), place(s) of residence, education, occupation, life and activities anchored by abundant dates; you want to provide insight into the creation of the materials. Always include a bibliographic citation for any background source you have used.

When describing an institutional body, the historical notes should discuss the body's founding and dissolution, its functions, activities, and relations with other units within the same institution, significant institutions, or units outside its home institution. You may need to include a summary of the most relevant aspects of the institution's history and existence, involving names of significant people or events, administrative structure, places of location or activities, and abundant dates to provide the context which produced materials. Again, always include a bibliographic citation for any background sources you use. DACS provides extensive direction in creating historical notes in its chapter 10.

Special Collections, Bailey/Howe Library, University of Vermont:
Bread and Puppet Theater Records, 1962–1985

The Bread and Puppet theater was formed by Peter Schumann in 1962, one year after its founder moved to New York from West Germany. In June 1970, part of Bread and Puppet moved to Plainfield, Vt., as theater-in-residence at Goddard College. In 1974 it moved permanently to Glover, Vt.

Since its beginning, the theater has been a small, self-managed, non-commercial theater committed to increasing people's awareness of social and political issues. Bread and Puppet is recognized throughout the world and has won distinction at international theater festivals in Italy, Poland, and Yugoslavia.

Louisiana and Lower Mississippi Valley Collections, LSU Libraries:
Hispanic American Collection, 1580–1940 (bulk 1810–1930)
Subseries 5. Frans Bloom Correspondence, 1928–1940, and miscellaneous correspondence, 1833–1842.

Frans Bloom was the director of the Middle American Research Institute at Tulane University. While in Mexico, Bloom corresponded with other noted archaeologists and anthropologists regarding archeological finds.

Custodial History or Provenance

ISAD(G)v2 rule: 3.2.3.

DACS element: 5.1.

EAD element: <custodhist>

RLG: R.

   Information about the hands the materials passed through from the time they left the control of the creator to the time they arrived at your repository gives the researcher insight into potential problems of authenticity and completeness. The custodial history should include dates of transfer from one "owner" to another. It should also include an explicit discussion of the ownership of intellectual property rights (i.e., copyright), whether they remained with a previous owner of the physical collection or have passed to your repository.

Department of Rare Books and Special Collections, Thomas Cooper
   Library, University of South Carolina Libraries:
   The John Abbot Watercolors, ca. 1795
   149 original watercolor paintings of Lepidoptera, the majority by
   John Abbot (1751–1840)
      On November 4, 1963, Sotheby's and Company of London sold
   these drawings to the rare book firm H.P. Kraus of New York City.
   According to the Sotheby's catalog (Lot 1), the drawings were
   previously the "property of a lady" who commissioned Sotheby's
   to sell the drawings on her behalf (3). Finally, the University of
   South Carolina procured the drawings from H.P. Kraus in 1964, and
   the drawings have resided in the Department of Rare Books and
   Special Collections at the Thomas Cooper Library ever since.

Acquisitions Information [ISAD(G)] or Immediate Source of Acquisition [DACS]

ISAD(G)v2 rule: 3.2.4.

DACS element: 5.2.

EAD element: <acqinfo>

RLG: R.

You need a record of the immediate source(s) of acquisition, including information on the method of acquisition, any terms agreed to as part of the process, the purchase price, if any, etc. Researchers may find some of this information highly useful. Undoubtedly they would find other parts interesting, if not actually useful for their purposes. Each repository will need to set a policy about which elements of information to share with researchers. While the standards expect you to collect the information, they offer no opinion as to whether you should make it public.

Special Collections, Bailey/Howe Library, University of Vermont:
Spear Family Papers, 1793–1942

The majority of the manuscripts in the Spear Family Papers came to the Wilbur Collection between 1978 and 1983. These acquisitions were part of the aftermath of a 1978 auction that dispersed the contents of the attic of Elhanan W. Spear's 1804 family homestead.

Scope and Content

ISAD(G)v2 rule: 3.3.1.

DACS minimum for single-level and multilevel description. DACS element: 3.1.

EAD element: <scopecontent>

RLG: M.

The scope and content section should provide enough detail about the content of the collection to allow the researcher to gauge its potential relevance. Without including the historical context, this section summarizes the activities that generated the materials; describes the documentary and intellectual characteristics of the materials; describes the persons, events, things, and phenomena to which records pertain; and includes the dates covered by the intellectual content, geographic areas to which the materials pertain, and any other information that might assist the researcher in determining the relevance of the materials.

Special Collections, Bailey/Howe Library, University of Vermont: Bread and Puppet Theater Records, 1962–1985

The Bread and Puppet Theater collection contains a wide variety of materials from the founding of the theater in 1962 to the present (1985). A large portion of the collection for each year consists mainly of correspondence which includes performance requests, job and participation inquiries, and personal letters.

Articles and reviews refer not only to Bread and Puppet, but sometimes to other similar alternative or experimental theater groups, as well as current social and political events that may have been incorporated as subjects of Schumann's plays. Flyers and advertisements are good examples of Peter Schumann's artwork; usually these are undated. Financial papers include account books, bills, salaries, receipts and grants.

The collection includes correspondence, contracts, schedules of performance and news clippings or reviews relating to the numerous European, Canadian and U.S. tours. There is also information regarding Goddard College, exchanges with other theater groups, addresses of members, friends and performance places. Several scripts and publications and a bibliography of films and publications about and by Bread and Puppet are in the collections. The bulk of the material is prior to 1980; correspondence, financial accounts and tour information are lacking for the later period.

A total of nine folders with photos of puppets are in the collection; some of the articles and reviews also have photos. There is also one tape cassette ("Insurrection Oratorio"—Carton III.)

In addition there are several untitled prints for productions abroad. Wood block prints were made by Peter Schumann using different colors, but mostly black and some red and blue. Some posters dated, others undated. There are various representations or prints for the same performances.

Louisiana and Lower Mississippi Valley Collections, LSU Libraries: Knute A. Heldner Papers, 1924–1978
Subseries 2. Drawings/Sketches, n.d. (.25 linear feet)
Summary: Subseries contains informal sketches completed by Heldner. Some drawings are interspersed with manuscript material. Several sketches appear to be studies for paintings. Other graphic material includes two Heldner prints, Heldner dry points printed on post cards and printed reproductions of Heldner paintings.

Appraisal, Destruction, and Scheduling Information

ISAD(G)v2 rule: 3.3.2.
DACS element: 5.3.
EAD element: <appraisal>
RLG: R.

Materials that come into historical repositories may lack true enduring value or may fall under the control of a records schedule. All repositories have formal or informal policies and procedures for removing this temporary material. If those policies apply to part or all of a collection, spell them out; include the rationale and the implications for the structure and use of the collection.

New Mexico State Archives:
  Requests for Legislative Memoranda and Bill Drafting
    Retention: permanent. After 15 years, transfer to archives. Ar-
  chives shall maintain records as a restricted collection.

Accrual Information

ISAD(G)v2 rule: 3.3.3.

DACS element: 5.4.

EAD element: <accruals>

RLG: R.

Not all materials in a collection arrive at the repository together. Institutional archives routinely add accruals to collections. When the repository
knows it will receive more materials for a collection, both researchers and
administrators should know what it expects to acquire, and, if possible, both
the volume and frequency of incoming materials.

Fictitious University
  Sue Ann Fictitious Papers
  Series III: Diaries
    Ms. Fictitious adds a new volume to this series each January.

Scheme of Arrangement

ISAD(G)v2 rule: 3.3.4.

DACS element: 3.2.

EAD element: <arrangement>

RLG: R.

In the arrangement process, archivists assign a physical and intellectual
order to a collection. Arranging a collection can amount to merely maintain-

ing the order imposed by the creator, it can require the archivist to create order out of chaos, or it can involve some of both. Regardless, researchers and staff both benefit by having the order described in the finding aid. When you describe it, include information about any series and subseries and their arrangements. Also include explanations of previous arrangements and/or reorganization if that might prove useful to either staff or researchers.

Special Collections, Bailey/Howe Library, University of Vermont:
Dorothy Canfield Fisher Papers, 1879–1958

Fisher's articles and stories (boxes 32-37) are arranged alphabetically by title, with untitled pieces at the end of the series (box 37) alphabetically by subject. Book manuscripts (boxes 37-64) are arranged chronologically in order to highlight Fisher's artistic development. Dramatizations (box 65) are arranged chronologically. Introductions DCF wrote for the works of others (box 65) are listed alphabetically by author. Reviews written by DCF, but not as a part of her Book-of-the-Month Club Activities (box 66), are also arranged alphabetically by author. Critical Studies of Fisher's work (box 66) are arranged alphabetically by author. Newspaper reviews (boxes 68–69) of her work are arranged chronologically. Photographs (boxes 69–70) are arranged alphabetically by subject. Miscellaneous items (boxes 70–72) are arranged alphabetically by subject.

Louisiana and Lower Mississippi Valley Collections, LSU Libraries:
United Confederate Veterans Association Records
Subseries 2. Adjutant Generals' correspondence, 1891–1941

Material is maintained in alphabetical order by generals' name, with the exception of George Moorman, William E. Mickle and Andrew B. Booth, which are maintained in chronological order by year.

Restrictions on Access [ISAD(G)v2] or Conditions Governing Access [DACS]

ISAD(G)v2 rule: 3.4.1.

DACS minimum for single-level and multilevel description. DACS element: 4.1.

EAD element: <accessrestrict>

RLG: MA.

A repository may restrict access to materials for a variety of reasons, including legislative or contractual restraints. The constraints may close a collection or a portion of it for a period of time, or they may impose a set of prerequisites the researcher must meet. Regardless, the nature and length of the restrictions, the source of the restrictions, and contact information for the person or agency authorized to handle an appeal of the restrictions should appear where both staff and researchers may find them.

DACS wants restrictions caused by problems with the condition of the materials to appear in its Physical Access element (4.2). ISAD(G)v2 allows it to appear here.

Henry Sheldon Museum of Vermont History, Middlebury Vt.:

    Stewart, Philip B. (Philip Battell)

    The Stewarts: Illuminated manuscript, 1993

       Restricted: The original may be used only by family members.

See librarian's file for definitions

Restrictions on Use and Reproduction [ISAD(G)v2] or Conditions Governing Reproduction and Use [DACS]

ISAD(G)v2 rule: 3.4.2.

DACS element: 4.4.

EAD element: <userestrict>

RLG: MA.

Even when researchers have access to collections, they may face limitations on how they may use or reproduce them. All limitations, including copyright restrictions, should appear in the finding aid as a way to remind staff and researchers of prerequisites that the user must meet.

Louisiana and Lower Mississippi Valley Collections, LSU Libraries:
Foster (Murphy J. and Family) Papers, 1880–1955 (bulk 1880–1930)
Restrictions: Use of personal correspondence between Murphy J. Foster and Mrs. Foster is restricted until July, 2023. Patrons may read this correspondence, but none of these letters may be reproduced, either whole or in part, without the express written permission of the donors or their heirs.

Language(s) and/or Script(s) and Symbol Systems

ISAD(G)v2 rule: 3.4.3.
DACS minimum for single-level and multilevel description. DACS element: 4.5.
EAD element: <langmaterial>
RLG: M.

Researchers will need to know whether they can read materials in a given collection, and so an indication of what languages and symbol systems a collection uses belongs in its description.

New Mexico State Records Center and Archives:
Records of the United States Territorial and New Mexico District Courts for Rio Arriba County, 1848–1954 (bulk 1848–1912)
Some materials in Spanish.

Louisiana and Lower Mississippi Valley Collections, LSU Libraries:

Uncle Sam Plantation Papers, 1815–1940 (bulk 1848–1911)

II. Correspondence, 1854–1911 (1.3 linear ft.)

Most of the correspondence in this collection is in French, the remainder being in English.

Physical Characteristics and Technical Requirements [ISAD(G)v2] or Physical Access [DACS]

ISAD(G)v2 rule: 3.4.4.

DACS element: 4.2.

EAD element: <phystech>

RLG: M.

Among older collections, the physical condition of materials may require restrictions to its access and use. Modern collections frequently contain data storage media which require specific technology for use, for storage, or for preservation. In all cases, the restrictions and technical specifications get spelled out here.

ISAD(G)v2 allows restrictions caused by the physical condition of materials to be included in its Access Restriction element, 4.3.1.

Fictitious University:

Sue Ann Fictitious Papers

Series I: Education, 1965–1988

Ms. Fictitious wrote her thesis on a DOS computer using WordStar 1.0 as her word processor. The disks containing her thesis require that program.

Other Finding Aids Available

ISAD(G)v2 rule: 3.4.5.
DACS element: 4.6.
EAD element: <otherfindaid>
RLG: O.

Finding aids come in many forms. In long-standing repositories they have evolved over time, and many collections have several types of finding aids describing various parts of the collection—some in great detail. Further, some collections have indices and other finding aids embedded in them. Researchers and staff alike will benefit by a notice that other finding aids exist. Indicate the type of information contained, the scope of the description, when it was created, and where it can be used. If a researcher may obtain a copy, include how to request one.

Henry Sheldon Museum of Vermont History, Middlebury Vt.:
Robinson family
Family letters, 1757–1962
Inventory, including genealogies, available at the Henry Sheldon Museum of Vermont History Research Center and at the Rokeby Museum, Ferrisburgh, Vt.

Existence and Location of Originals

ISAD(G)v2 rule: 3.5.1.
DACS element: 6.1.
EAD element: <originalsloc>
RLG: O.

Your repository may hold copies of original materials located somewhere else. The location of those originals should appear in the finding aid.

Louisiana and Lower Mississippi Valley Collections, LSU Libraries:
   Mignon (Francois) Papers, 1939–1970
      These reels of microfilm contain series 1, 2, and parts of 3 and 4 of
   the Francois Mignon Papers, a collection located at the Manuscripts
   Department, Southern Historical Collection, University of North
   Carolina at Chapel Hill. For a full description of the entire Mignon
   collection at UNC, including the series held at LSU on microfilm,
   see www.lib.unc.edu/mss/inv/htm/03889.html

Alternate Forms Available

ISAD(G)v2 rule: 3.5.2.
DACS element: 6.2.
EAD element: <altformavail>
RLG: R.

   Your repository may have the originals of a collection and know of copies
elsewhere. The location of those copies, and contact information for the repository, should appear in the finding aid. Alternatively, your collection may
have the only copies of a set of materials, but you may have them in a variety of formats, for example, paper originals and microfilm reproductions.
That information should appear in the finding aid.

Louisiana and Lower Mississippi Valley Collections, LSU Libraries:
   Mississippi River Map Collection, ca. 1858–1878
      Loose maps are also available on 6 CD ROMS.

Manuscripts Department Library of the University of North Carolina
   at Chapel Hill:
J. Mack Allison Papers, 1940–1966
Series 1. Personal Papers, 1940–1950.   10 items.
   The diary is also available on microfilm.

> Louisiana and Lower Mississippi Valley Collections, LSU Libraries:
>   Williams (T. Harry) Papers, 1775, 1861–1980
>   Series I. Correspondence, 1926–1980, n.d. (8 linear feet)
>   Originals of these letters are housed in the vault and copies are
>   filed by date.

Related Materials

ISAD(G)v2 rule: 3.5.3.
DACS element: 6.3.
EAD element: <relatedmaterial>
RLG: R.

No historical documents emerged from a vacuum, and both staff and researchers will benefit from knowing about other archival materials that have a historical or intellectual connection to those described in the inventory in hand. Those related materials may reside in the same repository or in another institution. Regardless, describe the relationship, including the title and location.

> Louisiana and Lower Mississippi Valley Collections, LSU Libraries:
>   Wright-Boyd Family Papers, 1812–1914
>   Related collections: David F. Boyd Family Papers, Mss. 99. Leroy S.
>   Boyd Papers, Mss. 99. Jesse D. Wright Papers, Mss. 99.
>
>
> Louisiana and Lower Mississippi Valley Collections, LSU Libraries:
>   Uncle Sam Plantation Papers, 1815–1940 (bulk 1848–1911)
>   III. Labor Materials, 1851–1911 (2.6 linear ft.)
>   Subseries 1. Tickets, 1896–1910 (1 linear ft.)
>   The materials from 1898–1911 indicate a close relationship between
>   payroll operations and the functioning of the Uncle Sam Plantation
>   Store, so researchers may wish to examine Series I as well.

> Rare Book, Manuscript and Special Collections Library, Duke University:
>   Charles W. Hoyt Company Records, 1894–1973, bulk 1909–1928
>   Hoyt Family Series, 1894–1973, and n.d.
>   Diaries Subseries, 1913, 1918–1919
>   *See also* Correspondence Subseries, Printed Material Subseries,
>   and Photographs Subseries of the Hoyt Family Series for materials
>   related to Camp Winnepesaukee.

Publication Note

ISAD(G)v2 rule: 3.5.4.

DACS element: 6.4.

EAD element:

RLG: O.

   If a previous researcher has published research based on or including use of a collection, both staff and researchers will benefit from knowing about it. Whenever possible, include bibliographic citations for those works about a collection or based on information contained in a collection.

> Louisiana and Lower Mississippi Valley Collections, LSU Libraries:
>   Wright-Boyd Family Papers
>   Group 1. Wright-Boyd Family Papers (1812–1914)
>   I. Correspondence, 1824–1913
>   Subseries 1. Wright family, 1824–1913
>   Correspondence from Augustus Wright (1853–57)
>   Part of this correspondence is reproduced in the typescript
>   "Greenwood Plantation and its People during the Civil War" Note.

Other Note

ISAD(G)v2 rule: 3.6.1.

DACS element: 7.1.

EAD element: <note> or <odd>

RLG: O.

The unpredictability of the collections we work with will forever remain one of the fascinating aspects of description of historical collections. But that very characteristic makes predicting everything that needs noting in the inventory impossible. Therefore, feel free to include notes that contain information that will help either the researcher or the staff.

Louisiana and Lower Mississippi Valley Collections, LSU Libraries: Lee (Russell) Photographic Collection

Another online source of information regarding the Russell Lee Collection housed in Southwest Texas State University's Wittliff Gallery of Southwestern and Mexican Photography is their website: www.library.swt.edu/wwc/wg/exhibits/rlee/index.asp

---

Archivists's Note [ISAD(G)v2] or Description Control [DACS]

ISAD(G)v2 rule: 3.7.1.

DACS element: 8.1.5.

EAD elements: <processinfo> and <descrules>

RLG: R.

Although processing typically happens out of the public's view, staff and administrators need a record of the steps and status of the processing of collections. Such information should be systematically collected for the work to continue smoothly. The record should include the names of people who worked on each collection or finding aid, the dates of the work done, the rules they followed in their work, and the sources they used to establish or

verify formats and information. Having this information systematically collected and recorded facilitates the systematic identification of materials which
may need a change or correction as human error appears or as standards
and "best practices" change. Typically this information does not appear as
part of the public record.

In the case of preservation and conservation measures, the information
may have an impact on the use or interpretation of the materials and should
appear in the finding aid.

University of Kentucky Manuscripts Archives:

Chinn (Asa C.) Downtown Lexington, Kentucky Photographic
Collection, 1920–1921

The original 8 x 10 nitrate negatives taken by Chinn were placed
in the archives. Years of improper storage before their placement in
the archives had resulted in nitrate negative decomposition, and
only 22 of the approximately 600 original negatives were in a state
that allowed images to be retrieved from them. Both traditional
contact printing and digital capture techniques were employed to
preserve their information. Due to the production of poisonous
gases and inflammable nature of degrading nitrate negatives, after
image capture or transfer, the negatives were safely destroyed.

Louisiana and Lower Mississippi Valley Collections, LSU Libraries:

Uncle Sam Plantation Papers, 1815–1940 (bulk 1848–1911)
I. Financial Papers, 1848–1911 (17.6 linear ft.)
Subseries 1. Checks and Bank Drafts, 1861–1911 (1.6 linear ft.)

Of the original 6 linear ft. of checks and bank drafts in the Uncle
Sam Plantation Papers, 1.6 linear ft. were retained after processing.
A sample of these checks and bank drafts was retained to reflect
accurately the role of fiat currency in plantation transactions. Several styles of checks were printed by banks during the fifty-year

> period 1861–1911. All checks and bank drafts from November and December of each year were retained as the representative sample.

Rules or Conventions

ISAD(G)v2 rule: 3.7.2.
DACS element: 8.1.4.
EAD element: <descrules>
RLG: O.

All archival description follows rules, standards, conventions, and protocols. This element provides a place to declare which of the above apply to the finding aid itself. It wants the name of the guide or guides that form the basis for the finding aid's structure and content, such as the *Rules for Archival Description* or ISAD(G)v2 plus *RLG Best Practice Guidelines*.

Dates of Descriptions

ISAD(G)v2 rule: 3.7.3.
DACS element: 8.1.5.
EAD element: <processinfo> with <p> with <date>
RLG: R.

ISAD(G)v2 calls for the date of processing as a specifically defined data element, while DACS incorporates it as a note describing accessioning, arranging, describing, and otherwise preparing the materials for use by researchers.

> Fictitious University:
>> Sue Ann Fictitious Papers
>> Series I: Education, 1965–1988
>>> This series was processed during the fall of 1995.

DACS Elements Not Specifically Addressed in ISAD(G)v2

Repository Name and Contact Information

DACS minimum for single-level and multilevel description. DACS element: 2.2.
EAD element: <repository>
RLG: M.

Of course you will start with your full legal name, but you might also include a statement that describes your placement in any larger institution that you support. In addition, the researcher would appreciate your address and other contact information.

> Department of Rare Books and Special Collections, Thomas Cooper Library, University of South Carolina Libraries, Columbia, S.C., 29208. Phone: (803) 777-8154. Fax: (803) 777-4661.
>
> Thomas Cooper Library's special collections are available to registered researchers in the Graniteville Room, entered through the mezzanine <www.sc.edu/library/mezzan.html> exhibit area.

An Abstract

DACS element: 7.1.2.
EAD element:
RLG: R.

An abstract of a couple sentences located on the front page of the finding aid will provide a clear statement of the essential nature of the collection and its context. Along with title and dates of the collection, the abstract helps the researcher to do a rough sorting out of useful collections and non-useful collections. DACS treats it as note, but EAD provides a tag for , so you might as well include one from the start.

Henry Sheldon Museum of Vermont History, Middlebury Vt.:
   Sons of Temperance of North America. Chimney Point Division,
   No. 35 (Addison, Vt.) Records, 1849–1853.
      A collection of minutes and financial papers of a fraternal organi-
   zation in Addison, Vermont, 1849–1853.

Preferred Citation

DACS element: 7.1.5.
EAD element: <prefercite>
RLG: R.

   A good citation explains exactly where a researcher found the evidence to
make the claim she or he makes, but the task of creating a proper citation for
original documents can strike fear in the heart of the even a seasoned researcher.
If you include in each finding aid the citation you prefer, you will not only give
the researcher the language and structure she or he needs, you will assure that
the citation includes all the information you will need to retrieve the material
for someone following the original researcher's footnotes.

Louisiana and Lower Mississippi Valley Collections, LSU Libraries:
   [Identification of item] Great Southern Lumber Company Collection (Mss. 3225). Louisiana and Lower Mississippi Valley Collections, LSU Libraries, Baton Rouge, Louisiana.

Separated Material

DACS element: 6.3.
EAD element: <separatedmaterial>
RLG: R.

   Frequently a collection comes to a repository containing items that do not
belong in an archival repository and that need removing. To maintain the

intellectual connection to their origins, describe the separated items in the finding aid. DACS and ISAD(G)v2 both include description of separated materials as part of the Related Materials elements, but EAD has a specific <separatedmaterial> tag for it, and you might want to segregate the information for that tagging.

Special Collections, Bailey/Howe Library, University of Vermont: Stone Family Papers, 1849–1998

Separated Materials: The following books and pamphlets were removed from Series V. and added to the general library collection:

Arthur Stone. *The First Hundred Years.* (duplicate) Fairbanks Weighing Division. [Booklet commemorating 150th anniversary of Fairbanks Scales.]

Wendell Phillips Stafford. *Dorian Days.* Inscribed "To Arthur Fairbanks Stone from Wendell Phillips Stafford, with grateful appreciation of his friendship. June 29, 1910."

Claire Dunne Johnson. *I See By the Paper: An informal History of St. Johnsbury.* Vol. I. Inscribed: "Wonderful reading!! Merry Christmas '87. Love, Claire" [probably Claire Moore]. Front page signed by the author.

A reminder: These elements do not represent the full EAD tag set. Since this book focuses on creating EAD-compatible finding aids on paper, none of the specifically computer or electronic-record related tags appear. If you focus on the content data elements listed here and scrupulously differentiate among them, you will have done what you can. The rest comes up when you move into an actual conversion project.

Notes

1. Steven L. Henson, "'NISTF II' and EAD: The Evolution of Archival Description," *American Archivist* 60 (Summer 1997): 286.

2. The need to publish these nested relationships online drove the development of EAD in the first place.

3. *Sample Forms for Archival and Records Management Programs* (Lenexa, Kans., and Chicago: ARMA International and Society of American Archivists, 2002).

4. Clay Redding, "Reengineering Finding Aids Revisited: Current Archival Descriptive Practice and Its Effect on EAD Implementation," *Journal of Archival Organization* 1:3 (2002): 35–50. Christopher J. Prom, "Does EAD Play Well with Other Metadata Standards? Searching and Retrieving Using the OAI Protocols," *Journal of Archival Organization* 1:3 (2002): 51–72.

5. You will find names and descriptions of specific standards scattered throughout this book, placed with the descriptive element each relates to.

6. Dennis Meissner, "First Things First: Re-engineering Finding Aids for Implementation of EAD," *American Archivist* 60 (Fall 1997): 372–387.

7. Redding, ibid.

8. A number of state and regional projects have also developed guidelines which you might consider, and which might serve you better in terms of your data's compatibility with a local union database. The RLG project welcomes materials from all across the country, however.

9. www.loc.gov/ead/tglib/index.html.

Chapter 5

Putting It All on Paper

The developers of DACS and ISAD(G)v2 understood that all the descriptive practices one might want to apply to the full collection could prove valuable at subordinate levels. Therefore they built into EAD the power to reuse most of the data elements at all levels within the inventory. EAD does not restrict the archivist's ability to describe the materials in a collection, or to apply retrospective conversion to even the most detailed collection. Feel free to describe collections as fully as they need. But recognize that working on paper has encouraged certain habits and has certain requirements that you need to think about. Further, as long as you work on paper you will want to continue conventions that paper inventories need but which you know will probably not migrate to the screen—conventions such as tables of contents, running heads, page numbers, etc. To continue those conventions for as long as you work on paper while preparing to convert to EAD, you will want to set up routines to use with your word processor file so that the conversion from paper to screen goes as effortlessly as possible.[1] This chapter will address those issues.

Creating Container Lists

Highly detailed and long container lists entice those who create them to indulge in practices aimed at speeding up creation of the inventory. While those shortcuts serve the purpose in the moment, and while most researchers can follow their meaning in a paper document, some will lead to problems in conversion to EAD. While efficiency mechanisms may appear in all areas of a finding aid, they occur most densely in box/folder lists.

Mechanism 1: Abbreviations

When confronted with the need to enter the same proper noun hundreds of times in the course of developing an inventory, what archivist can resist the urge to reduce obvious names to an abbreviation? (See the Auld correspondents list in chapter 1.) However, the archivist looking ahead to data conversion understands that a computer's search engine will not translate abbreviations in an online inventory the way a researcher's brain will. The savvy archivist will avoid them. The really savvy archivist might use abbreviations in creating the word processing file that becomes the inventory, but will expand the abbreviations through one or more search-and-replace maneuvers before calling the document complete.

Mechanism 2: Ditto Marks

Do not expect to use dittos in an EAD document. Knowing that information remains permanently fixed on a page, archivists can type one full line of text at the top of a page and then repeat the information using only ditto marks for the rest of the entire page, if necessary. The researcher will always see that page as a set unit until she or he turns the page.

Computers, however, do not deliver permanently fixed information. In 2004, most computer screens display about twenty-five lines of text from anywhere in the text. What may at one moment appear as the last line on the screen may instantly move to the top line as the text rolls up the screen. The screen will display any twenty-five consecutive lines in the file, scrolling equally easily from front to back and back to front. Imagine the uselessness of a screen of ditto marks, and, in that environment, the frustration it would generate. The savvy archivist uses exactly the same operation with dittos that he or she applies to abbreviations, that is, she or he uses them to lessen the time needed to key in the original document, and then, like abbreviations, expands them as she or he finishes.

Further, a search engine cannot interpret a ditto mark. The ability to do computerized searching is one of the great advantages of an electronically published inventory. Loading such a document with ditto marks destroys that ability.

Bear in mind, however, that dittos serve a function on paper that abbreviations do not. The white space around dittos allows the researcher to focus on new information provided by the words interspersed among the dittos while she or he almost subconsciously applies the dittoed information as she or he reads. Endless repetition of information undeniably clutters up a printed page. Since the computer screen does not display as much information as a page, the screen will not seem as busy as the page, but it will undoubtedly have some crowded quality. A well-designed stylesheet will diminish that to some degree.

If you do not want to load up the printed page with dozens of repetitions of a phrase, preferring to stay with the abundant white space dittos produce on printed documents, create two versions of the file by copying the ditto-ridden file to a new file. Expand the dittos in one and set it aside for EAD-Day.

Tables of Contents

A paper inventory needs a table of contents (TOC) at the very beginning to provide an overview of the structural sections of the inventory and page numbers for each section. The Web also relies on TOCs as navigational aids. On the screen, Web TOCs appear in two ways. In the first, the table sits at the top of the document and links to sections within it.

If your conversion moves your inventories to this structure, the paper version of the TOC, without its page numbers, will serve the same purpose.

Another method, however, has the computer copy text from the document itself for display on a small portion of the computer screen, usually on the left.

The computer generates the two TOC formats in two completely different ways. If your conversion moves your inventories to the side-by-side structure, the paper TOC will serve no purpose and need not be converted to electronic format.

Word processors give you two ways to create a TOC. You can create one by hand, that is, analyze the document and hand-key the TOC at the top of the file or on another page. Alternatively, most programs allow you to embed TOC code into the word processing file. When you have finished adding the code, the program will generate the TOC for you. For example, the embedded code to create a table of contents entry in WordPerfect is set off like this: {Mrk Txt ToC} code 1} Table of Contents (TOC) {/Mrk Txt ToC: 1}.

If you use the first method, create the TOC as a separate file or create it at the top of the inventory. It makes no difference. If you embed codes, however, think ahead. At conversion time, you will need to go back to the word processing file and remove all that coding. With that in mind, the savvy archivist will not embed TOC codes as she or he creates the inventory. She or he will complete the inventory first and save the completed file without the codes, anticipating using it as a clean file for conversion. The archivist will then copy the clean file to a working file, embed TOC codes into the working file, and use that one as the print version. *Caveat:* If you have two versions of a single file, remember to update the content of both if you update the content of one. Otherwise, you no longer have two copies of one file, but two different files.

Narrative Descriptions

Good inventories have a section of narratives near the front to provide the context of the collection through biographical and historical information on the creators. The narratives may fill a single paragraph or many pages, and having them collected at the front of the inventory as an overview of the entire collection falls exactly within the ISAD(G)v2 specifications. Problems arise with similar contextual materials for subordinate units of the collection. Paper documents force readers into a more or less linear progression from front to back. In a paper world, it serves the reader well if you bring the series level biographical and historical information, as well as the scope and contents, of various series to the front also. Reading through these narratives, the researcher can get an overview of the collection followed by an overview of the series and subseries within it. Having found the area of greatest interest, the researcher can then go to the container list for more detail. Collecting these descriptive narratives at the front relieves the scholar from searching through the pages of container lists of one series to find descriptions of the next one.

However, electronic documents do not work on a linear model. In an environment of hypertext links, placing the historical sketches and scope notes at the head of the level they describe makes more sense than collecting them at the front of the inventory. A hyperlink can take the researcher from the TOC to a subordinate unit, and the scrolling feature of the screen will allow the researcher to scroll easily from the contextualizing material to the container list.

With this functional difference in mind, you could set up your inventory's word processing document for conversion relatively easily in two ways. First, you can create the word processing document so it prints out as you would like, knowing that when conversion comes, those series and subseries narratives will need moving further down in the file. Alternatively, you can insert the information into the electronic document where you will want it to appear on the screen (i.e., with the materials it refers to), then adjust the inventory's page numbering so you can pull the narrative pages out of their print-out position and arrange them according to the page numbers.

Example: Suppose you have a thirty-page inventory of which five pages contain descriptions of the five series in the collection. You could collect those descriptions at the front of the document and print them out on pages 8 through 12. Come conversion time, someone may want to move those pages so they display at the head of the container list of materials each describes. That could mean moving the text within the file or programming the stylesheet to appear to move it.

Alternatively, in the word processing file, you could put the text at the head of the container list for each series description. Figuring out that, if printed at the beginning of the file, these descriptions would fill pages 8 through 12, you manipulate the word processor to number the first description as page 8, the second description as page 9, the third as page 10, etc. This also involves manipulating the pagination before and after it. Having done that, however, when you print the document out for addition to your collection of paper finding aids, you simply pull the pages from their place in the printed document and insert them into the document according to their page numbers.

Both methods require a fair amount of forethought and attention to detail. If the collection will likely receive new accessions, the page numbers will need to be adjusted every time new descriptive matter appears in the inventory. In that case, better efficiency probably lies in moving data at the time of conversion, either by hand or through some electronic magic connected with displaying it. If, however, you know a collection will not grow, placing the narrative with the container list for the documents it describes and adjusting the page numbers makes the most sense.

Chronological Lists

Biographical and historical information may appear as a narrative, a chronological list, a table of events, or a combination of them all. If you include a chronological list, place the dates on the left. EAD coding of chronological lists insists on it. If a chronological list has dates on the right, converting from paper to EAD will require reversing the two columns. The format simply will not accept chronological lists with dates on the right.

[INCORRECT] Vermont AAUW State Presidents

Elizabeth Isham	1920–1921
Ellen Cramton	1921–1922
Ellen Ogden	1922–1925
Marion Gary	1925–1929

[CORRECT] Vermont AAUW State Presidents

1920–1921	Elizabeth Isham
1921–1922	Ellen Cramton
1922–1925	Ellen Ogden
1925–1929	Marion Gary

Mixed Data

Before archivists had to factor the needs of computers into their descriptive practices, they looked for ways to provide as much information as they could as compactly and graciously as possible. Explanations like the following examples have many virtues related to useful information, compactly presented in a graceful manner. Unfortunately, these explanations blend data elements, which will make them slower and more costly to convert to EAD. By creating good clear differentiation of your data elements, you will speed EAD conversion significantly.

The examples below show the text as it appears in the original inventory. The EAD tagging shows how, without changing the text, an encoder would isolate the data elements to facilitate EAD conversion.

Louisiana and Lower Mississippi Valley Collections, LSU Libraries:
Israel L. Adams Family Papers, 1813–1890

Merchant farmer from Natchez, Mississippi, and his family from northeast Louisiana. Collection consists of letters, bills, receipts, printed items, with most correspondence written after Israel's death (1860), between the children Frank O. Adams and Kate, as well as between related members of the Adams, Zingline and Shupan families. Most items originate in Adams County, Mississippi and Tensas Parish, Louisiana. Subject matter varies, with Civil War letters forming a unified topic; manuscript volume (1860–62) contains notations on the I.L. Adams estate. Xerox copies of funeral notices and miscellany in im

---

<bioghist>Merchant farmer from Natchez, Mississippi, and his family from northeast Louisiana.</bioghist> <scopecontent> Collection consists of letters, bills, receipts, printed items, with most correspondence written after Israel's death (1860), between the children Frank O. Adams and Kate, as well as between related members of the Adams, Zingline and Shupan families. Most items originate in Adams County, Mississippi and Tensas Parish, Louisiana. Subject matter varies, with Civil War letters forming a unified topic; manuscript volume (1860–62) contains notations on the I.L. Adams estate.</scopecontent> <altformavail>Xerox copies of funeral notices and miscellany in impr.</altformavail>

Biographical Information: Merchant farmer from Natchez, Mississippi, and his family from northeast Louisiana.

Scope and Content: Collection consists of letters, bills, receipts, printed items, with most correspondence written after Israel's death (1860), between the children Frank O. Adams and Kate, as well as between related members of the Adams, Zingline and Shupan families. Most items originate in Adams County, Mississippi and Tensas Parish, Louisiana. Subject matter varies, with Civil War letters forming a unified topic; manuscript volume (1860–62) contains notations on the I.L. Adams estate.

Other forms available: Xerox copies of funeral notices and miscellany in impr.

University of South Carolina Libraries Rare Books & Special Collections, Thomas Cooper Library:
The John Manners Iggulden Papers, 1983–2001
    Materials in the collection have been donated by the author himself over several years. The papers provide an important key to the

intersection between Iggulden's life and his various works. The papers are supported by a collection of Iggulden's published books,
donated by Professor Matthew J. Bruccoli.

  <acquinfo>Materials in the collection have been donated by the
author himself over several years.</acquinfo> <scopecontent>The
papers provide an important key to the intersection between
Iggulden's life and his various works.</scopecontent>
<relatedmaterial> The papers are supported by a collection of
Iggulden's published books, donated by Professor Matthew J.
Bruccoli.</relatedmaterial>

  Source of materials: Materials in the collection have been donated
by the author himself over several years.
  Scope and content: The papers provide an important key to the
intersection between Iggulden's life and his various works.
  Related materials: The papers are supported by a collection of
Iggulden's published books, donated by Professor Matthew J.
Bruccoli.

University of South Carolina Libraries Rare Books & Special Collec-
  tions, Thomas Cooper Library:
The James Willard Oliver David Hume Collection
  The collection was formed by Prof. James Willard Oliver (1912–
2001). Prof. Oliver (Ph.D. Harvard 1949) taught at the University of
Florida and at the University of Southern California before moving
to the University of South Carolina in 1964, as Professor and first
Head of the new Department of Philosophy. Through Professor
Oliver's generosity, his Hume collection was transferred to the Uni-
versity in 1997. In the following years, Prof. Oliver also transferred

his substantial collections of works by and about Bertrand Russell (1872–1970) and of modern American logic, notably the logic of W. V. Quine (1908–2000), with whom Prof. Oliver had worked at Harvard.

<origination>The collection was formed by Prof. James Willard Oliver (1912–2001).</origination> <bioghist> Prof. Oliver (Ph.D. Harvard 1949) taught at the University of Florida and at the University of Southern California before moving to the University of South Carolina in 1964, as Professor and first Head of the new Department of Philosophy.</bioghist> <acquinfo>Through Professor Oliver's generosity, his Hume collection was transferred to the University in 1997.</acquinfo> <relatedmaterial>In the following years, Prof. Oliver also transferred his substantial collections of works by and about Bertrand Russell (1872–1970) and of modern American logic, notably the logic of W. V. Quine (1908–2000), with whom Prof. Oliver had worked at Harvard.</relatedmaterial>

Souce of Materials: The collection was formed by Prof. James Willard Oliver (1912–2001). Through Professor Oliver's generosity, his Hume collection was transferred to the University in 1997.

Biographical Information: Prof. Oliver (Ph.D. Harvard 1949) taught at the University of Florida and at the University of Southern California before moving to the University of South Carolina in 1964, as Professor and first Head of the new Department of Philosophy.

Related Materials: In the following years, Prof. Oliver also transferred his substantial collections of works by and about Bertrand Russell (1872–1970) and of modern American logic, notably the logic of W. V. Quine (1908–2000), with whom Prof. Oliver had worked at Harvard.

Special Collections, Bailey/Howe Library, University of Vermont: Charles Phelps Papers, 1754–1785

The University of Vermont purchased the Phelps collection from the Brooks Memorial Library in Brattleboro, Vermont, in 1973. The Brooks Library, the Vermont Historical Society, one private collector in Vermont, and the Porter-Phelps-Huntington Foundation of Hadley, Massachusetts, also have collections of Charles Phelps manuscripts. In the 1870s James H. Phelps, who donated his ancestor's library and manuscripts to the Brooks Library, published some Charles Phelps documents in Volume Three of Records of the Governor and Council of the State of Vermont, E.P. Walton ed. (Montpelier: J. & J.M. Poland, 1873–80): 490–98.

<acquinfo>The University of Vermont purchased the Phelps collection from the Brooks Memorial Library in Brattleboro, Vermont, in 1973.</acquinfo> <relatedmaterial>The Brooks Library, the Vermont Historical Society, one private collector in Vermont, and the Porter-Phelps-Huntington Foundation of Hadley, Massachusetts, also have collections of Charles Phelps manuscripts.</relatedmaterial> <altformavail>In the 1870s James H. Phelps, who donated his ancestor's library and manuscripts to the Brooks Library, published some Charles Phelps documents in Volume Three of Records of the Governor and Council of the State of Vermont, E.P. Walton ed. (Montpelier: J. & J.M. Poland, 1873–80): 490–98.</altformavail>

Source of Materials: The University of Vermont purchased the Phelps collection from the Brooks Memorial Library in Brattleboro, Vermont, in 1973.

Related Materials: The Brooks Library, the Vermont Historical Society, one private collector in Vermont, and the Porter-Phelps-Huntington Foundation of Hadley, Massachusetts, also have collections of Charles Phelps manuscripts.

> Alternative Forms: In the 1870s James H. Phelps, who donated his ancestor's library and manuscripts to the Brooks Library, published some Charles Phelps documents in Volume Three of Records of the Governor and Council of the State of Vermont, E.P. Walton ed. (Montpelier: J. & J.M. Poland, 1873–80): 490–98.

Running Heads and Page Numbers

Typists routinely create running heads and footers that keep the researcher oriented in the finding aid and the collection. While highly valuable in a paper document, the computer screen may have no use for these running heads and footers. To avoid having to remove them from the body of the inventory file, create a header or a footer through a function of the word processor. Using the program's routine will allow you to delete the header or footer with a single command, instead of having to manually delete each one from each page.

Internal vs. Public Information

DACS and ISAD(G)v2 would have you put all information in one place—the finding aid. Regardless of whether you have your inventories on paper or in an electronic file, you will need to decide how much of the information you want to share with the public. In the paper world, you will need to separate the pages of internal information from the pages of public information. In the electronic world, you can keep the information all together and, through the stylesheet, simply instruct the computer to display only some of it to the public.

As you develop your finding aids with a word processor, consider including all the information in the file. If you put all the internal information on one or more pages together, after printing out a paper document you can file the pages of internal information away from the public. If you have adjusted your pagination well, researchers will not notice the absence of those pages. The efficiency of having all the data together when you want to convert argues for this approach.

Other Notes

The unpredictability of the collections we work with will forever remain one of the fascinating aspects of processing historical collections. But that very characteristic makes predicting everything that needs noting in the inventory impossible. Therefore, feel free to include notes that contain information that will help either the researcher or the staff. EAD has an element called Other Descriptive Data, <odd>, for just such information. Never withhold information from the inventory because you cannot quite figure out where to put it within the structure outlined above. Do, however, separate it from other data elements and identify it as "Other Descriptive Data." At conversion time it will stand out as needing <odd> tagging and not run the risk of inadvertently winding up somewhere else.

Document Your Decisions

Working in the world of paper while anticipating the electronic world calls for lots of creativity and thought about what you will need to do in the future and how you can get set up today to make conversion as easy and efficient as possible. Once you have done all that creative work, take credit for it. Write it down so your successors know what you have done and why. Writing the report is never as much fun as creating the solutions, but it is necessary. Without good documentation, your successors will get lost, and your work will end up a frustrating shambles. Take the time to document your decisions.

Note

1. This book assumes that the inventory has become the basic finding aid and it uses language that reflects that assumption. The reader should know, however,

that EAD will support other formats. It also assumes that you present inventories on paper, whether you generate them from a database, a word processor, or a combination of both.

Chapter 6

Intellectual Access
and Information Retrieval

When a patron approaches you at the reference desk and asks about materials relating to the Great Depression, you face two distinct information retrieval tasks. First you must identify those collections that address the need. You do that through finding aids of many sorts—sifting through your memory, checking an old card catalog, searching through one or more online catalogs or databases, looking through lists that organize holdings by topic, talking with your colleagues, looking through inventories, etc. Second you must identify where the appropriate collections reside. For that you turn to a location device of some variety.

The second task involves physical access—knowing where to go to get the collections you want. The first involves intellectual access—identifying those collections that relate to the question. You can assure good physical access through a well-maintained locator list. Intellectual access takes more work.

The drive to standardize archival description comes from the need to enable information retrieval through computers. Computers excel at manipulating data, but they have a very hard time understanding it. If asked to find everything about Elizabeth Dow, a computer will match the letters as they appear in the request statement. It probably will not know that Elizabeth Dow has papers calling her Elizabeth H. Dow, but it could probably find them. However, I spent a couple decades as Mary Elizabeth Hicks and have used the nickname Wiz[1] all my life. If the humans entering data into the record do not add that information, the computers probably will not find papers using those names. Remember, for all its apparent sophistication, a computer is as dumb as a hubbard squash. It will always do what we ask, but it has no understanding of what we want. Making it do what we want requires a lot of human effort. The larger the project (and creating computer-searchable databases of archival finding aids is *huge*), the more work people must put into it. Archivists' grand vision of creating union databases of archival inventories requires a tremendous amount of work and discipline from all the humans involved, just so the computers can do what they do well. Much of the work revolves around the need for intellectual access. Good information retrieval depends on good intellectual access.

The publication of finding aids and primary documents on the World Wide Web has brought together in one file the methods and perspectives of two traditional ways of providing intellectual access to historical materials: creating a surrogate for the material and creating a map to the contents of the material. Document surrogates, such as catalog cards and MARC records, describe the essential characteristics of the materials, both physically and intellectually. Document maps, like the standard back-of-the-book index, do not try to describe whole documents; they provide specific access points to people, places, concepts, ideas, and events (i.e., details of the content). Archivists have used both methods. We have created catalog cards and MARC records as collection-, series-, and item-level surrogates, but we have also created lists, calendars, and indexes to provide maps to our materials.

Inventories do all of the above. EAD, as a protocol designed primarily for inventories, brings all traditions together. The use of controlled vocabularies and precise tagging allows the researcher to identify and retrieve the information in inventories much faster and more easily than she or he could ever expect of a collection of paper inventories.

The computer's capacity to identify terms in many documents using a variety of logical relationships means that your EAD-encoded finding aids become a virtual database, accessing the computer's ability to search every word of the document to provide intellectual access. As you mark up your finding aids, keep in mind that you are really building a database in which every word becomes an access point—a point that gives you access to the information you seek. Traditionally, book users think of author, title, and subject for their access points. Users of historical documents may think of the creator, but they frequently ask for a type of material (letters, diaries, etc.), occupation (railroad worker, secretary, etc.), place and/or time of origin (nineteenth century Texas, etc.). Historical documents have a formal title much less frequently than published documents, but when one does exist, it too becomes an access point, as does the title provided by the archivist.

Tagging for Intellectual Access

EAD and other electronic publishing systems have built the needs and capacities of computers into their design. Without special programming, a run-of-the-mill computer search engine will find all occurrences of the term "snow" in a document or database of records, but it will not distinguish between Matthew Snow, a person; Snow's Market, a corporation; Mount Snow, a geographical location; or a snow fall, a meteorological event. However, tagging in electronic documents provides the code the computer needs to distinguish one use of a term from another. We can tag Matthew Snow as <persname>Matthew Snow</persname>, and, with a good search engine, the searcher can request all occurrences of the term "snow" as a <persname>, eliminating all the other uses of the term. An electronic text with sophisticated markup, and a sophisticated search engine, gives the searcher the choice of full-text searches or searches for specifically tagged data. So, good practice means you do not mix data within tags. A searcher could ask the computer to return information from the <bioghist> tag or the <scopecontent> tag and expect to get very different types of information. Notes on restriction to access, <accessrestrict>, and restrictions of use, <userestrict>, refer to two different situations, and we support our researchers by tagging them differently.

Controlled Vocabularies for Intellectual Access

Consistent, reliable intellectual access benefits enormously from standard-izing or controlling the vocabulary of access points. Controlled vocabularies have provided library patrons with a uniformity of terms that makes using a library a fairly predictable experience, regardless of size or location. Fur-ther, controlled vocabularies made possible the merging of the records of holdings of thousands of individual items into databases that provide ac-cess to the holdings of many—in some cases hundreds—different institu-tions. For the scholar, controlled vocabularies provide some assurance that a limited number of terms will identify all useful material. In the form of name authority files, controlled vocabularies identify the persons, corpo-rate entities, places, events, concepts, etc., referenced in a work, regardless of how the official name or natural language may have changed.

When archivists started using MARC to add their records to library data-bases in the late 1980s, they confronted for the first time the need for con-trolled vocabularies and names. Less than two decades later, we are still sorting out the details. Consider the following example.

In the autumn of 1999, these entries appeared in the index of a database that specializes in American history. The numbers to the right of the name indicate the number of times each version of the name appears in the data-base.

> *McClellan, George B. (17)*
> *McClellan, George Brinton (67)*
>
> *Manassas (2d battle) (2)*
> *Manassas (battle) (1)*
> *Manassas (Bull Run; battle) (1)*
> *Bull Run (2d battle) (26)*
> *Bull Run (2d campaign) (2)*

We can see the controlled terms the database producers prefer, but we also see how often variants appear. Unless programmed specifically to collect all those variations when a patron asks for any one of them, the search engine will give the patron only what she or he asked for—not what he or she wanted. Any term that does not specifically match the requested term will not appear. Therefore, as computers become more central to the way we store and retrieve information, the need for us to provide them with consistent data grows. As the archives profession develops union databases for finding aids, the need for controlling names grows, and it is not easy to accomplish. After all, if a single database producer has trouble controlling vocabulary within its own organization, imagine the chaos that may result from blending the creations of hundreds of organizations if they do not adopt the same standard. Consider this: in December 2004, the Research Libraries Group Archives Resources, a union database of online finding aids and MARC records, contained about 49,500 finding aids from 192 contributors.[2]

Search engines developed for commercial Web searching, such as Google, do not rely on controlled vocabulary. Instead they use various formulas for the mathematical probability that one word in relation to another word addresses the question inherent in the query statement. Indeed, in this early part of the twenty-first century, various projects to develop metadata-based markup and retrieval protocols bespeak a fundamental skepticism about the possibility of ever fully implementing retrieval through controlled vocabulary systems.[3] The developers of these metadata projects and search engines may or may not succeed in making controlled vocabulary completely irrelevant. The prudent archivist will not bet on their success. Instead, the prudent archivist will understand that controlled vocabulary in a finding aid will never hinder a powerful search engine, and it will aid a crude one.

EAD specifically provides for four types of names: personal names, family names, corporate names, and geographical names. It also provides a universal name tag. We will deal with each in turn.

Personal and Family Names: <persname> and <famname>

How did the most prominent of the nineteenth-century town clerks in Hardwick, Vermont, spell his name? A search of the ArcCat database at the

University of Vermont will show that, as a young man of business, he spelled it Alden J U D E V I N E.[4] However, as town clerk during the middle of the century, he spelled it both Alden J U D E V I N E and J E U D E V I N E in the town records. After his death in the late 1880s, his widow built a library building to honor him and a son who had died young. She had it named the J E U D E V I N E Memorial Library. [5] Alden Jeudevine illustrates a ubiquitous issue in historical documents: spelling, especially the spelling of names. We have no universal standard for spelling family names. No rule book says that you must spell the family name Chesnutt, C H E S N U T T, and that you may not spell it C H E S N U T or C H E S T N U T. In the case of Alden Judevine/Jeudevine, the spelling makes no real difference. You could choose one and standardize around it. In other cases, various spellings of a single name may have significance as a way to distinguish among several families. You may want to use them all. Some standards have evolved for some individual names, and if one exists, you should use it in your effort to establish intellectual access. In all cases, record your decision.

Start looking for standardized names by going to large authority files. You will find a rich store of authorized names at the Library of Congress. You can access their databases through their website,[6] and you should use it whenever you can. Unfortunately most of the local notables that small repositories collect do not appear in the Library of Congress Name Authority File (LCNAF).

If the names you need do not appear there, or anywhere else, establish a form of each person's name using chapter 12 in DACS which conforms with the International Standard Archival Authority Record for Corporate Bodies, Persons and Families (ISAAR(CPF)). DACS will serve as a guide for what to include and how to form the record.[7] Record the name you have established, other forms of the name, or other names the person used. Indicate the sources from which you got the name you will use. Use it consistently.

Creating an authority control system like the one discussed above will unquestionably prove expensive in the personnel time it will require. Consider working with other repositories which have collections like yours to develop a union list you all share. Collaboratively you can decide who truly counts as a "local notable" for inclusion into the file and what form the name you will all use should take. Collaboratively you can decide who will do what work.

The Vermont Archival Network (VAN), an informal collaborative of archivists in northern Vermont that came together more than a decade ago, developed a union database, called ArcCat, of MARC records for their manuscript collections.[8] To keep the database as clean and user-friendly as possible, the VAN participants developed a list of standard forms for the names of local notables whose papers reside in several repositories around the state but which do not appear in any of the national lists. Everyone uses the standard version of the name in their finding aids, although the name might appear in many forms and several spellings in the actual papers. VAN members meet regularly to discuss issues they all share, including the name authority file.

For more than a decade, the Library of Congress has used its Program for Cooperative Cataloging (PCC) to tap into the knowledge and records that exist in repositories all over the world.[9] While the total PCC program goes beyond the name authority program to include subject authority, bibliographic records, and serials, NACO, as they call the name authority program, has the most to offer archivists, and they have the most to give back. Under NACO, local catalogers, trained by LC, may submit names to the LCNAF. According to the NACO annual report for 2003, in that year 247 NACO institutions contributed 167,163 new name authority records, bringing the total to more than two million contributed by local repositories. Those contributions have swelled the LCNAF to over five and a half million authority records.[10] The savvy archivist will notice two things. First, LCNAF has more local names than one might think; always check it first. Second, becoming a NACO affiliated institution can mean that your work becomes available for the rest of the world to share.[11]

Corporate Names: <corpname>

From the beginning of time, corporate names have changed frequently—maddeningly. DACS establishes rules and guidelines for standardizing corporate names in chapter 14, including what to do when they change. The LCNAF provides you with the authorized name for hundreds of corporations which have operated in North America, as well as a history of the name changes each corporation has undergone. If LCNAF does not contain a corporate name, DACS and ISAAR(CPF) rules will guide you in creating an authorized name and an authority record to support it.

Geographic Names: <geogname>

Geographic names remain more stable than corporate and personal names, but they too change. DACS will guide you in choosing and formatting geographic names in chapter 13, and the Getty *Thesaurus of Geographic Names* (TGN) has become a popular authority source.[12] The thesaurus contains a million place names (and growing) including historical and variant names. It also provides basic location data.

Other Names: <name>

Lots of things besides people, places, and corporations have names. Rather than clutter up the tag set with myriad tags related to names, EAD creators provide one general purpose tag for the rest. The *EAD Tag Library* suggests you use <name> when you do not know for sure what type of name you are working with. Does a reference to "a trip to Snow's" refer to the market or the family? EAD prefers the use of the general tag rather than mistagging with one of the more specific tags. However, for the sake of future tag-based searching, try to be as specific as possible.

Caveat: Distinguishing between a place name and a corporate name may not be as intuitive as it seems. In a letter in which the writer refers to his wife as being at the asylum, the reader probably thinks of a place. Technically, however, an asylum is a corporate entity, and if you tag the asylum, you should tag it <corpname normal="Asylum Name">the asylum</

corpname>. Is a castle a place or a corporate entity? What about London Bridge? You can always fall back on the general <name> tag, but you can also check the list the Library of Congress has created to help you make the distinction.[13]

Using Attributes with Names

Attributes in markup languages provide a way to add controlled terms to documents. All the EAD tags discussed above have an attribute NORMAL, intended as a way to add a controlled form of a name. Take Mary Fish for example.[14] Born in Stonington, Connecticut, in 1736, Mary Fish became Mary Noyes in 1758, when she married John Noyes. Noyes died in 1764, and ten years after Noyes' death, she married Gold Selleck Silliman and became Mary Silliman. Gold Silliman died in 1790, and Mary married John Dickinson in 1804. She lived as Mary Dickinson until her death in 1818. In a database, how do you keep her straight from all the other Marys that populate her enormous family connection? Obviously you must pick a name for her, but which one? Well, LC has settled on Silliman, Mary Fish Noyes, 1736–1818. Gold Silliman served as a leader in the Connecticut militia during the Revolutionary War. In addition, the Silliman children and their children had a long and sometimes distinguished connection with Yale, making the Silliman name the most prominent and recognizable of those Mary bore. The LCNAF authority record for her does not even mention Dickinson. So, imagine you are the archivist working with the papers of her final widowhood. She has become Mary Dickinson, but you need a way to connect her back to Mary Silliman. It is easy in EAD:

```
<unittitle>
     <persname normal="Silliman, Mary Fish
     Noyes, 1734–1818">Mary Dickinson</persname>Letters,
</unittitle>
<unitdate normal="1815"> 1815</unitdate>
```

By embedding the "normalized" version of the name in the tag, you have assured that a computer could find it easily. On paper, however, having both could be trickier. Certainly you would explain name changes in the biographical notes. In addition, regardless of what the folder titles say, you could prepare lists of normalized names used in the collection. At conversion time, these lists would get tagged as part of the various <controlaccess> sections. With these lists of controlled names, you have a choice later about normalizing data in, for instance, folder lists which use a nonstandard form of a name. Alternatively, you could use only standard forms in the finding aid, regardless of the actual content of the material.

Subject Headings for Intellectual Access

EAD provides the tag <subject> for those topics associated with or described by the materials in a collection. Like names, the terms should come from a standard thesaurus. The Library of Congress Subject Headings (LCSH) represents a commonly used general vocabulary, but certainly not the only one. The number of discipline-based thesauri ballooned with the development of online bibliographic databases in the 1970s and 1980s. Many, however, go back to the nineteenth century.

When you add subject headings to an inventory, you may either collect them in one place or scatter them throughout the document—EAD can handle either method. In the first example below, you will see how you might indicate controlled names and how they would later be coded in EAD. When you work on paper, be sure to record the authority you use. If you had to create authorized terms, be sure to indicate the standard you used. If you record this authority information in the paper finding aid itself, the information will never get lost. When the time to convert arrives, your successors will not need to search beyond the document in hand to determine the authority you worked from, and they will thank you for your foresight.

Bear in mind that <controlaccess> will also accommodate subject entries and thus encourages a form of indexing on paper. Treat your subject terms like names: use standard terms, record the source, and be consistent.

Subjects

> All personal, family, and corporate names conform to the authorized form maintained in the Library of Congress Name Authority File online. If LCNA did not hold the name at the time this document was created, it conforms to the authority list maintained by the Vermont Archival Network. Place names conform to the Getty Thesaurus of Place Names. Names not found in standard name authorities have been created according to DACS guidelines and maintained at this institution. Topical terms came from the Library of Congress Subject Headings, #th edition.

People

> Judd, Eben W. (Ebenezer Warner), 1761–1837

Organizations

> Essex Community Players

Places

> Essex Junction (Vt.)

Topics

> Theatre—Vermont

After conversion, the coding could look like this. Though the tagging would remain invisible to the user, a search engine would find it.

```
<controlaccess><list><head>Subjects</head>
    <note>All personal, family, and corporate names conform to the
    authorized form maintained in the Library of Congress Name Au-
    thority File. If LCNA did not hold the name at the time this docu-
    ment was created, it conforms to the authority list maintained by
    the Vermont Archival Network. Place names conform to the Getty
    Thesaurus of Place Names. Names not found in standard name au-
```

thorities have been created according to ISAAR(CPF) guidelines and maintained at this institution. Topical terms came from the Library of Congress Subject Headings, #th edition.</note>
<item>
  <list><head>People</head>
    <item><persname source="van" >Judd, Eben W.
    (Ebenezer Warner), 1761–1837</persname></item></list>
</item>
<item><list><head>Organizations</head>
  <item><corpname source="lcna">Essex Community
  Players</corpname></item>
</list></item>
<item><list><head>Places</head>
  <item><geoname source="gnt">Essex Junction (Vt.)
  </geoname></item>
</list></item>
<item><list><head>Topics</head>
  <item><subject source="lcsh">Theatre—Vermont</subject>
  </item>
</list></item>
</list>
</controlaccess>

EAD allows you to leave your controlled terms embedded in the text of the inventory. If you choose this method, you will want to do all the authority control while you create the inventory and note the source(s) you use. For example:

Container List
        All personal, family, and corporate names conform to the authorized form maintained in the Library of Congress Name

Authority File. If LCNA did not hold the name at the time this document was created, it conforms to the authority list maintained by the Vermont Archival Network. Place names conform to the Getty Thesaurus of Place Names.

Carton 2 Folder 33 New England Foundation for the Arts, 1993
Carton 2 Folder 34 New England Foundation for the Arts:
    Successful Grants, 1997
Carton 3 Folder 28 Action for Franco-Americans in the Northeast
    (ActFANE), 1994
Carton 3 Folder 29 Celebration of Women Festival, 1994

After conversion, the markup could look like this.

```
<container type="box">Carton 2</container><container
   type="folder">Folder 33 </container> <unittitle><corpname
   source="lcnaf">New England Foundation for the Arts,
   </corpname> <unitdate>1993</unitdate></unittitle>

<container type="box">Carton 2 </container><container
   type="folder">Folder 34 </container> <unittitle><corpname
   source="lcnaf">New England Foundation for the Arts,
   </corpname>: Successful Grants, <unitdate>1997
   </unitdate></unittitle>

<container type="box">Carton 3 </container><container
   type="folder"> Folder 28 </container><unittitle>
   <corpname  reg="Action for Franco-Americans in the Northeast"
   source="van"> ActFANE: </corpname> Franco-American Group,
   <unitdate>1994</unitdate></unittitle>

<container type="box">Carton 3</container><container
   type="folder">Folder 29 </container> <unittitle><corpname
   source="van">Celebration of Women Festival,
   </corpname><unitdate> 1994</unitdate></unittitle>
```

Each method has advantages. Collections with controlled vocabulary aggregated in a standard place at each level will convert more easily. If you have the terms aggregated at one spot, you can develop a relatively simple program or template to automate the conversion from just text to marked-up text.

Collections with controlled vocabulary scattered throughout the container list will require a fairly sophisticated—probably custom-made—program to automate and even then will require a lot of human intervention. However, scattering controlled terms throughout the document will allow a search engine to mark its "hits" and identify them exactly in context.

If you convert all your names to authorized forms in all uses, you could forgo tagging them as personal names, corporate names, etc., knowing that a search engine would find them during a full-text search. However, leaving them untagged could prevent a tag-based search from differentiating Snow from Snow.

As you can tell, these decisions have real consequences. You do not want to make them lightly. In large measure you must weigh the benefits of creating something that search engines can take advantage of in the future against the staff-time you have available today. Undoubtedly you will want to do as much as you can, but whether you do the maximum or the minimum, do it consistently. Your successors can figure out and successfully work with whatever you do, as long as you do it consistently. A good computer programmer can create automated routines to handle highly repetitive work with data that has a predictable structure and format. You want to provide your successors' programmers the highly predictable structure and format to work with.

To repeat: you, the prudent archivist, cannot start too early in developing the controlled vocabulary and standardized names for your inventories. Good tagging, combined with good vocabulary control, provides a very powerful (because it is precise) search query.

One more thing. If you now "index" your inventories with something that resembles a back-of-the-book index, do not link the indexed terms to the page of the inventory; use the series or box or box/folder numbers or any other way of identifying the relevant materials. You could move these terms into a <controlaccess> tag or use the <index> tag in EAD, designed for that type of list. However, electronic documents have no pages to refer to. If you reference page numbers, after conversion the reference will have no meaning. If you reference box/folder numbers, or other specific places in the inventory, it will.

Notes

1. My older brother—age three when I arrived on the scene—couldn't say Liz, and the grandmother for whom I was named Elizabeth preferred Wiz to Liz or Lizzy.

2. Gregory Whitfield.,RLG Project Manager, in a private e-mail message to me, November 23, 2004.

3. In August 2002, RLG held a half-day forum on metadata and its use in cultural heritage institutions. At that time, presenters discussed five projects under development: www.rlg.org/events/metadata2002/.

4. arccat.uvm.edu/.

5. hardwickvtarea.com/Hardwick/library.htm.

6. authorities.loc.gov.

7. Created by the same organization that created ISAD(G), it provides a detailed description of all the information needed for an authority record, www.hmc.gov.uk/icacds/eng/ISAAR(CPF)2.pdf. If you want to post your list of authorized names online, use the Encoded Archival Context (EAC) protocol to mark it up, found at xml.coverpages.org/eac.html.

8. www.vermonthistory.org/arccat/repos.htm.

9. loc.gov/catdir/pcc/2001pcc.html.

10. loc.gov/catdir/pcc/annualrpt03.html.

11. NACO: www.loc.gov/catdir/pcc/naco.html.

12. www.getty.edu/research/conducting_research/vocabularies/tgn/.

13. loc.gov/catdir/pcc/saco/alpha405.html.

14. Joy Day Buel and Richard Buel, Jr., *The Way of Duty: A Woman and Her Family in Revolutionary America* (New York: Norton, 1984).

Chapter 7

Starting Your EAD Collection

Up to now, this book has focused on what you should do to create finding aids that convert easily to EAD—sometime in the future. Now it will look at what putting those inventories on the Web will actually require.

Your EAD work will affect every facet of your repository's arrangement and description function, as well as its information technology. The savvy archivist starts by getting political buy-in from all the departments the work will touch. Given the cooperation and resources required to mount an EAD program, you must have the support of the whole institution (i.e., administrators at all levels) and as many staff workers as possible. Everyone must understand why your institution has decided to do this and how it expects to benefit from it. Everyone needs a sense of ownership and commitment. When you have that, you can get down to the myriad details and decisions. You can start thinking about the program in a number of places, but as it evolves, you will need to examine all of the factors below.

Factors to Consider

Who Will Make Crucial Decisions, and How?

This question relates to the buy-in issue. The nature of any particular decision will determine who makes it, but if you think of *policy* decisions that address issues the staff in the program face on a routine basis, then you have a number of choices.

1. The "boss," whomever that might be. You could have one or two people managing the project and making all the major decisions about it.
2. One or more committees wielding authority over all or specialized domains.
3. All involved personnel constituting a committee of the whole.

There is no right answer to this question, any more than to any other question posed here. But there is a wrong answer, and that is to not think about the process before you get into the middle of it. As you work through the rest of the questions below, think about who should make the decisions and what the decision-making process should entail.

Which Finding Aids Will You Encode?

How will you choose the finding aids (not just inventories—EAD can handle any number of styles) you will encode? What priorities will you set? Start by thinking about what types of finding aids you have. Along with traditional inventories, you may have various lists of holdings, an old catalog containing standard library-type card catalog records, and other types of guides, like indexes, calendars, etc. You may have notebooks which have similar information. You may have a collection of MARC records which have collection- and series-level records for collections. From these various candidates, which will you choose? Only you can determine the right answer, and you may not even have to struggle with it. But you need to make a conscious decision before you start planning the work; your decisions will shape all aspects of the actual work. For example, a project set on pulling a hierarchically related assortment of MARC records into a single document will need very different tools and support than a project to convert a collection of paper inventories. The following criteria come to mind as possibilities:

1. Everything you have. If that is the decision, you need to decide on an order for their conversion.
2. Everything you now have in an electronic format. If you have been

creating finding aids by word processor for a number of years, you may decide to mark them up and not rekey the ones that exist only on paper. Again, you still need to decide the order in which you will convert them.

3. The finding aids that get the most use, or the finding aids for the collections you get the most calls for, or the finding aids for collections of most interest to researchers from afar.

4. The finding aids for the materials with the highest interest to the broadest spectrum of people.

5. Finding aids for those materials you know to have high historical value but which get low use for whatever reason.

6. Finding aids that people ask for, either to answer in-house needs or to serve researchers who make specific requests.

7. Easy ones—finding aids that meet high standards and will need little adjusting to suit current best practices.

8. Only those finding aids you create after you have done a thorough rethinking and redesigning of your finding aid format to suit current understanding of best practices.

9. Finding aids on subjects for which grant funding might enable you to carry out some of your fondest dreams—including EAD conversion.

As you see, you can base your decision on lots of rationales. In the end, your decision about your priorities depend on your institutional needs and goals; they will reflect what will serve you best.

What Markup Guidelines Will You Follow?

You will want to establish markup guidelines to ensure a consistent look and feel in the style of your EAD publications. Which one will you choose? Will you create one of your own? Will you reengineer your inventory style in the process? This book suggests you adopt the RLG *Best Practice Guidelines* because they relate to a program that covers the whole nation. Regional guidelines exist (e.g., the Online Archives of California *Best Practice Guidelines*), which you might adopt. Only you can decide where to get your guidelines, but you must decide. Do not get halfway into the work and wish you had paid more attention to certain details about your markup—details a set of guidelines would have alerted you to.

Who Will Do Your Markup?

A number of data conversion companies will encode finding aids for repositories. They charge by the number of characters and guarantee a high level of accuracy in the documents they produce. Most of them send the actual work offshore to companies that have large populations of low-wage, educated, English-speaking workers, places like India and the Philippines. Such companies provide a real service for those institutions that do not have and do not want to develop the in-house staff to do the encoding themselves.

Hiring a firm to do your encoding will spare you that actual work. It will not spare you any decisions about the coding. These firms work to your specifications. They may have suggestions, but in the end, all decisions remain yours. The data service probably will advise you to "clean up" your data—expand abbreviations and dittos, normalize names if you want, etc.—before you send it. Unless you also go through the data and make the intellectual distinction between <bioghist> and <scopecontent>, it will not get done. In an effort to save money and speed up the conversion from type to electrons, you can undermine the distinction of intellectual components that EAD makes so readily distinct. Finally, when you receive your data back, you may have additional modifications to make. The data service probably will not create your stylesheets for you. If you decide to do your encoding in-house, you will need people to do it, and tools to facilitate it.

How Much Perfection Will You Strive For?

Envision a continuum of practices: at the perfection end you rework all your finding aids (and perhaps reprocess collections) so they meet your best practice guidelines perfectly. At the other end, you willingly and knowingly misuse the EAD tag set just to get the work on the Web. Few institutions have the time and staff to commit to perfection. Equally few will perpetrate bad markup for the sake of speed. Most find a comfortable place in the middle. EAD's flexibility will accommodate a wide variety of solutions to the problems, but the closer you stick to your guidelines, the better your data will play with others.

Where Will You Learn Your EAD?

If you decide to do your encoding in-house, you will need to learn as much about the technology as you can. Working with EAD means working in an XML environment, which means learning to work with stylesheets as well as the markup. Working with EAD means learning the tag set and its internal working requirements and relationships. Your software can help keep you out of trouble, but it will not advise you about what you probably should do next.

You can learn on the job—ultimately you *will* learn *a lot* on the job—but getting some training can make that a faster process. You should look into the two-day workshop offered by the Society of American Archivists. Additionally, the Rare Books School, located at the University of Virginia, offers several week-long classes on how to work with electronic publishing and specifically with EAD. If you live near a college or university with an archives education program, you could look for a class there. You could hire a consultant to act as a private tutor and troubleshooter. You could volunteer at a local institution that has an EAD program in progress. There are lots of ways to learn the protocols you need to know, and you need to give yourself and your staff the time and space to do it.

What Tools Will You Need?

1. Access to *all* the standards manuals and guides we have discussed in the previous chapters.
2. The Society of American Archivists publications relating to the implementation of EAD: *The Tag Library* and *The Users' Guide*. While you will find both, free, on the SAA website,[1] when you start your program you will want to buy the books; they are much more convenient to use.

3. An XML editor, like XMetal or oXygen—programs that can read the technical files and guide you in your work or allow you to create a template into which you can enter data. XML editors work very much like word processors, and most have a "parser" which will tell you if you have created good markup that an XML-aware browser will read. You will want to have one of these whether or not you do the bulk of your own markup. It will help with the pre- and post-markup tweaking.

4. Some customized programs, while a luxury for many, can make the difference between a process that proceeds like a glacier and one that clips right along. This book is dedicated to the programmer at the University of Vermont who took truly daunting repetitive tasks and turned them into work a freshman could do with virtually no training. We could not have done the job without him.

5. If you cannot find a programmer who can work with you, look into the *EAD Cookbook*, developed by Michael J. Fox of the Minnesota Historical Society and available for free on the EAD Help Pages website at the University of Virginia.[2] It has made the process as close to "cut and paste" as possible. Similarly, the Online Archives of California has a toolkit and set of best practice guidelines available to the public.[3]

6. A subscription to the EAD Listserv.[4] While not an especially busy list, it keeps EAD users in touch with the latest developments. Occasionally it will carry a discussion of the best solution to a problem a user has.

How Will You Handle Privacy and Confidentiality Issues?

We all have finding aids that indicate that we have records that hold information that might violate someone's privacy—employee records in one of our corporate collections. While the evidence of these records sat in paper finding aids in an institution with set and limited hours located in one specific place on the face of the planet, we could rest comfortably knowing that relatively few people would "stumble across" the information and make merry or mischief with it. Put that same information on a universally accessible medium that is open at all hours to anyone with an Internet connection and a browser, however, and it gives one pause. Only you can decide whether and how to display such evidence about your collections, but you need to make a decision about it.

A slightly different twist applies to closed materials, especially whole collections that have been closed. Will you acknowledge them or wait for them to come open before posting the finding aid to the Web?

How Much Intelligence Will You Add?

Tagging represents an addition of intelligence to inventories, as chapter 6 explored. It can, therefore, provide an enormous help to the researcher. But it takes staff time to research and apply the tags. You will need to make a decision about the level of tagging you will apply, whether you will apply the same amount regardless of the collection involved or perhaps vary it depending on the historical importance of the materials. If you vary it, you will need to know what level applies to what collection, based on what criteria.

The same applies to normalization of names and dates. RLG would have you normalize all dates, but leaves names and <controlaccess> terms to your discretion.

How many layers deep will you take <controlaccess> terms? EAD allows you to add <controlaccess> at all levels. How minutely will you apply this sort of indexing to the people, places, things, events, and concepts in your collections?

How Will You Publish Your Materials?

Do you have a server and the technical staff to do the publication in-house? If not, who will host your site? What requirements will they place on you? Any maximum file size? Any schedule for feeding them the files to publish? You want to work out lots of details like this as one of the first things you do—even if your department relies on another department in your institution.

If you publish your EAD documents in XML, straight out of the XML editor with stylesheet attached, bear in mind that browsers older than those published around 2000 probably cannot read them. To make sure that everyone can read them, you could publish in HTML, but that means dumbing down your XML to HTML, which adds an extra step to your publication process. Alternatively, you can assume that eventually the world will catch up to you and post in XML.

How Will You Organize Your Site?

Look ahead to the future when you have succeeded in putting up a couple hundred inventories. Do you have them listed in one great alphabetical order, or have you organized them into groups? What kind of groups? It may seem early to think about this, but as you are designing the website on which you will post your EAD-encoded documents, you might want to design it now to accommodate such a plan, so you avoid having to redesign it later. Take the time to develop an understanding of good website design. Spend some time looking over lots of other repositories' sites and notice what works and what doesn't. Consult your users. Consult others' users. As with most things, the more thought you put into your basic organizational plan in the beginning, the less you will need to worry about it in the future.

What Kind of Search Capability Do You Want to Provide?

A number of the Web search engine companies will supply you with a version of their product to enable local searches. Do you want to provide that? How powerful do you want the engine to be? Having invested all this time and energy into creating highly intelligent data, do you want to provide researchers the ability to take advantage of that intelligence by, for instance, enabling tag-based searching, that is, specifying that a search confine itself to certain tags, such as <persname> or <bioghist>? Do you want the ability to assist researchers by creating templates to aid their searching in sophisticated ways they may not be aware of? Take the time to test as many search engines as possible, making notes of everything you like, dislike, or might like if it were available.

Before you go shopping for a search engine, create an image of what the prefect one would do and how it would return the data to the user. Delve into the studies of users of archival resources[5] that have begun to appear and see what you can learn about what researchers want from archival materials or what they find confusing about using archives and online finding aids.

Who Will Do the Work?

You will need someone to manage the work, someone to oversee data conversion and/or creation, one or more people to do the actual markup, and someone to do the Web publication. Those jobs could all be done by one person, or you could develop a whole team of people. Regardless, you will need to decide where the people will come from. Will you hire new employees? Will you use people already on staff? Perhaps a combination of new and in-house personnel?

If you use in-house people, what work will they cease to do? Will your institution just stop doing that work, or will you hand it off to someone else? Who? Perhaps you will hire someone to do the work of a staff member who would like to work on the EAD conversion. However you plan to get the work done, do not assume you can merely add it to your current staff's job descriptions.

Where Will People Work?

Everybody has to be somewhere, and everyone has a supervisor. If you bring new people into your offices, where will you put them and their equipment? Nearly everyone doing this work will need a computer; do you have space for them? Will they report to you, or will another department in your institution supervise them? If they do report to another department, you and their supervisor must reach an understanding about what decisions you will make and what will remain in that department.

How Will You Keep Track of the Workflow?

Marking up a finding aid in EAD involves a lot of steps. If you have more than one person working on the program, you will need to plan how the work will flow among workers, how much time each step will need, and who will do each. How will you change the workflow plan if the initial plan does not work?

How Will You Handle Quality Control?

You will want to build in quality controls for each step. While you cannot perfect this system until you have some experience, you can see the need and anticipate some of the problems before you get started. For example, if you have decided to normalize all dates, then you know you will need some way to check the normalization, at least initially. Further, your software will tell you if your markup actually is wrong, but it may have a hard time telling you exactly what is wrong about it.[6] You may want to designate someone as the proofreader for all obstinately wrong markup. While the software will evaluate the markup, it will not respond at all to the content data. How will you make sure it is "authorized" and well formatted? If you have adopted a set of best practice guidelines as your model, you will want a person or program to check compliance. Other issues will surface as you do the work.

How Will You Keep Your Files Straight?

Every XML document uses at least two files—the marked-up file and the stylesheet. You may find you develop a number of others, like word processing files and image files. Be aware from the very beginning that the way you name your files can help or hinder your work. The savvy archivist will develop a system for naming files that indicates the content of each (the file extension serves this function well to distinguish between different types of files—.txt, .doc, .xml, .jpg, etc.) and the relationship among files. Your system may need some adjustment over time, but several years out, wouldn't you like to look at a file name and know—based on its name only—where it fits in the project, even if you no longer remember the inventory it relates to?

How Will You Support This Program?

Know from the beginning that you will need to commit to regular updating of your hardware and software. If you control the server that holds your files, you can have some say in the timing of that process. If, however, you have found another host for your files, you will need to work within the rules of that shop. Expect periodic migration of your data and software. Insist on it.

How Will You Handle the Additional Requests These Generate?

Having your finding aids on the Web will generate requests for service from people all over the world who find them. How will you respond? Consider creating a dedicated e-mail address to receive such requests (include it in the contact information in your electronically published documents) and establish workplace rules for making sure requests get handled promptly. Give this a lot of thought. Will you promise a response within a certain time limit, for example, 24 hours? Will you set limits as to how much work you will perform for e-patrons? Will that vary from one e-patron to another? If so, on the basis of what criteria? Libraries have offered e-reference services for a few years now, and you might spend some time reading through the literature looking for good ideas about what makes a successful e-reference site for both the patron and the provider.

How Will You Pay for All This?

The most fundamental question of them all. You will need start-up money for hardware, software, manuals, training, etc. You will need operating expenses for the cost of salaries and additional materials. While this question appears in last place on this list, you will want to address it first. The questions above give you an idea of what to factor into your budget.

Retrospective Conversion and Legacy Data

Retrospective conversion—reconning—of old finding aids will eventually force you to consider every finding aid anomaly possible. It will tax your patience and provide you with well-earned "highs" after you have solved a problem. It will force you to confront all your fuzziness about how and why your institution creates finding aids and how and why you want to change them. But before you get to that level of fun, you must make the same decisions you have made above, and you have one more decision unique to reconning: How much unification do you want among those collections which have multiple finding aids?

Your older inventories may include bibliographies, file plans, indices, notes on separated materials, additional materials, or how a particular collection relates to other holdings in your own repository or others' repositories. EAD allows you to continue to create those cross-references—even encourages it. But, as with all elements in your new finding aids, it wants you to create those sections as discrete units. As you look through older finding aids, look for ways to segregate different types of information that the creator may have integrated into a single statement. Look especially closely at long narratives at the beginning of the finding aid. You may find lots of different types of information presented as a flowing essay of information for the researcher. Similarly, you may find that container lists, written as a single list, actually contain materials that today you would collect as a number of series. In other words, when it comes time to recon an older finding aid, you may not need to rewrite it, but you need to rearrange it by breaking up these essays into discrete, labeled paragraphs and dividing the container lists into series.

In the end, if you have descriptive matter that does not seem to fit neatly into any of the data fields we discussed earlier, do not despair. EAD has a tag for Other Descriptive Data <odd>. Do not throw information away because you cannot now see where it might fit EAD. You can tag it <odd> and just explain it for what it is. <Odd> allows you to lift blocks of quotes from the old finding aid and create tables and lists of structured data or paragraphs of narrative. Use it as a last resort, but do not be afraid to use it.

You may have one or two large important collections which have a variety of different finding aids. For example, the following are finding aids for the papers of Successful Q. Gathergold, Esq.:

1. A file box of Gathergold's speech titles and organizations addressed, arranged by date, created by Gathergold's secretary between 1925 and 1955.
2. List of "Correspondents in the Gathergold Papers," created in 1969 by Ernest Volunteer.
3. List of "Photographs in the Gathergold Papers," created in 1972 by Ernest Volunteer.
4. "Successful Gathergold Papers," an inventory created in 1975 by Early Archivist.
5. "Index to the Gathergold Papers," created in 1980 by Latter Archivist.

EAD can absorb many different types of lists and inventories for retrospective conversion. Start now, though, developing a model of how those multiple forms of access will relate to one another. In the case of the Gathergold materials, you could use the 1975 inventory as the basic document. To it you could add the file box index to speeches by converting it to a chronological list containing the date, the title, and the organization names.

```
<dsc>
  <c01><did><unittitle>Speeches,</unittitle>
    <unitdate normal="1925-1955">1925-1955</unitdate>
    </did><otherfindaid><chronlist>
    <chronitem><date normal="1925-08-13">August 13, 1925
    </date><event>Tyrone Rotary Club: "Mentoring the
    Next Generation."</event></chronitem>
    <chronitem><date normal="1945-10-27">October 27, 1945
    </date><event>Tyrone Kiwonis Club: "Now that the War
    is Over."</event></chronitem>
    </chronlist>
    </otherfindaid>
  </c01>
</dsc>
```

You could then add the list of correspondents, also as a chronological list.

```
<c01><did><unittitle>Correspondents,</unittitle>
  <unitdate normal="1930/1975">1930–1975</unitdate>
  </did>
    <otherfindaid>
    <chronlist>
    <chronitem><date normal="1930-07-19">July 19, 1930
    </date>
    <event>Ephraim Fromme to Successful Gathergold
    </event></chronitem>
    <chronitem><date normal="1932-12-12">December 12,
    1932 </date>
    <event>Successful Gathergold to Sarah Quick
    </event>
    </chronitem></chronlist>
    </otherfindaid>
  </c01>
```

The list of photographs could appear as a part of the normal hierarchy, occasionally containing a more specific list.

```
<c01><did><unittitle>Photographs</unittitle>
  <unitdate normal="1925/1975">1925–1975</unitdate>
  </did>
  <c02><did><container type="box">Box 1
  </container><container type="folder">Folder 1
  </container><unittitle>Vacation in the Gatineau, Quebec
  </unittitle><unitdate normal="1932-08">August, 1932
  </unitdate></did>
  <list>
```

```
      <item>Fishing boat</item>
      <item>The "Lodge"</item>
      <item>The day's catch</item>
      </list>
      </c02>
   </c01>
```

Furthermore, if you did the authority work on the names, you could tag the authorized version as part of the controlled access vocabulary.

```
<dsc>
   <c01><did><unittitle>Speeches,</unittitle><unitdate nor-
   mal="1925/1955">1925–1955</unitdate></did>
   <chronlist>
   <chronitem><date normal="1925-08-13">August 13, 1925
   </date><event><corpname normal="Rotary Club (Tyrone,
   Pa.)">Tyrone Rotary Club</corpname>: "Serving as a Men-
   tor to the Next Generation."</event></chronitem>
   <chronitem><date normal="1945-10-27 ">October 27, 1945
   </date><event><corpname normal="Kiwanis Club (Tyrone,
   Pa.)">Tyrone Kiwanis Club</corpname>: "Now that the
   War is Over."</event></chronitem>
   </chronlist>
   </c01>

   <c01><did><unittitle>Photographs</unittitle><unitdate
   normal="1925/1975">1925–1975</unitdate></did>
   <c02><did><container type="box">Box 1
   </container><container type= "folder">Folder 1
   </container><unittitle>Vacation on <geoname>Lac
   Lapeche
```

```
    </geogname> in <geogname normal="Gatineau, Parc de
la"> the Gatineau</geogname></unittitle><unitdate nor-
mal="1932–08">August, 1932</unitdate></did>
<list>
<item>Fishing boat</item>
<item>The "Lodge"</item>
<item>The day's catch</item>
</list>
</c02>
</c01>
</dsc>
```

You could do the same for the index. Given that you will have pulled all this information together into one file, you may find that you do not need to repeat information on which the various paper formats overlap. Or you may. Your decision will reflect your resources and the uses you know the collection will receive. EAD does not care.

You could decide to tag all these finding aids as discrete files and then hyperlink them. EAD puts sophisticated linking tags at your disposal.

Finally, once you commit to standards-based EAD compatibility, insist that all new inventories comply with it. If you start to apply EAD-think to your inventories now, you will minimize the conversion that will face you or your successors in the future.

Your Title Page

Title pages have become popular for finding aids on the Web. On paper or on the Web, title pages provide an attractive first impression for the researcher using your site, as well as an overview of the collection. Look over the model title pages located at these URLs; you may find an idea for something you can do on paper.

Harvard's Online Archival Search Information System:
oasis.harvard.edu/html/sch00077frames.html

Manuscripts Department, Library of the University of North
Carolina at Chapel Hill: www.lib.unc.edu/mss/inv/htm/
20010.html

Ohio Historical Society: www.ohiohistory.org/resource/
archlib/collections/msscoll/mss991/title.html

Bryn Mawr College Library Special Collections:
www.brynmawr.edu/library/speccoll/guides/
cozens.shtml

Oregon State Archives Department of Forestry Records:
arcweb.sos.state.or.us/state/forestry/forhome.htm

Notes

1. www.archivists.org.

2. jefferson.village.virginia.edu/ead/cookbookhelp.html.

3. www.cdlib.org/inside/projects/oac/.

4. To subscribe, see www.loc.gov/ead/eadlist.html.

5. "Special Section: Users and Archival Research," *American Archivist*, 66 (Spring/
Summer 2003): 9–101; Paul Conway, *Partners in Research: Improving Access to the
Nation's Archive* (Pittsburgh: Archives and Museum Informatics, 1994).

6. Most XML editors come with a program that will check markup against the
rules embedded in the coding scheme. Some provide information that makes
correcting errors easy; others do not.

Glossary

This glossary includes terms relating to archival description, information management, and electronic publishing *as used in this book*. Many of the terms here have other meanings in other disciplines and contexts; those meanings do not appear here. The glossary relies heavily on the definitions developed in *A Glossary for Archivists, Manuscript Curators, and Records Managers*, by Lewis J. Bellardo and Lynn Lady Bellardo; *The Organization of Information*, by Arlene Taylor; as well as a variety of other sources.

Access Point

Names and subject terms chosen by an archivist to assist information retrieval. In an electronic system, any term used in the document can serve as an access point which a computer uses in information retrieval.

ALS

Autograph letter, signed. A handwritten letter signed by the author.

APPM

Archives, Personal Papers, and Manuscripts, by Steve Hensen. APPM served as the content standard for archival cataloging between 1983 and 2005.

Archives

The non-current records of an organization or institution preserved for their continuing value.

Arrangement

The organization of historical documents in accordance with archival principles.

Attribute

Terms embedded into a markup element to further define the text the element describes.

Authority Control

The process of establishing one authorized term for use when several different terms might apply equally well.

Authority Data

Data relating to all aspects of authority control.

Authority File

A group of authority records.

Authority Record

The record which holds all the decisions made in the process of establishing an authorized term.

Bibliographic Database

A collection of bibliographic records describing books and/or journal articles held within a database. Such databases in great number became commercially available to scholars, for a fee, in the 1970s.

Calendar

A chronological list of individual documents.

Collection

1) A body of historical materials relating to an individual, family, or organization. 2) An accumulation of materials devoted to a single theme, person, event, or material format, brought together by a collector.

Component

A segment of the description of an archival collection (e.g., a series, a file, or an item).

Container List

A listing of materials in one or more containers.

Contextual Information

Information about the origins of a particular set of historical documents.

Controlled Vocabulary

A standardized list of terms used to represent concepts known by a variety of terms, for example, "American Civil War" for any of the twenty-six titles the conflict has received.

CSS

Cascading Style Sheet. A stylesheet language for formatting the appearance of information on a computer screen.

Curator

A person with responsibility for acquiring and managing historical collections in a manuscripts repository.

CUSTARD

Canadian-U.S. Task Force on Archival Description. An international committee which worked for several years to develop a North American standard for archival description. Though it did not achieve its stated goal, CUSTARD resulted in major revisions of the basic archival descriptive guidelines used by both nations.

DACS

Describing Archives: A Content Standard. Publication representing the most recent American iteration of the contents of archival descriptions. DACS grew out of U.S. participation in CUSTARD as a replacement for APPM.

Data Content

Synonym for Data Value.

Data Element

A discrete type of information, such as title, creator, or biographical note.

Data Format

The look of the content of a data element.

Data Structure

The way data elements relate to one another to create a full record.

Data Value

The information that fills a data element.

Description

The process of establishing intellectual control over a group of historical documents.

Descriptive Standard

A rule or body of rules that control description.

EAC

Encoded Archival Control. An XML protocol for encoding authority records.

EAD

Encoded Archival Description. An XML protocol for encoding archival finding aids.

EADWG

EAD Working Group. An SAA committee charged with oversight of EAD.

File

In ISAD(G)v2, the third level of description; the smallest cohesive unit of materials in a collection of historical documents.

Finding Aid

A descriptive tool that provides physical and/or intellectual control over a group of historical documents.

Format

In electronic publishing, the "look and feel" of text as it appears on the screen.

Full Text Database

A database of complete documents, as opposed to a bibliographic database, which contains only bibliographic citations to documents.

Function

In electronic publishing, the role a segment of text plays (e.g., title, unique identifier, historical note).

Hierarchical Arrangement

An arrangement of archival materials which organizes them from the largest aggregate level through intermediate aggregates down to an item level.

Historical Repository

An agency or program responsible for the acquisition and care of historically significant materials so that the materials provide evidence or information accessible to the public.

Holdings

All documentary materials in a historical repository.

HTML

A markup protocol for publishing simple brochure-like documents on the World Wide Web.

ICA

International Council on Archives. The ICA is the professional organization for the world archival community dedicated to promoting the preservation, development, and use of the world's archival heritage.

Index

A systematically arranged list providing access to a finding aid.

Information Retrieval

The process of finding desired information from a store of information, either print or electronic.

Information Retrieval Protocol

The established rules for using any particular information retrieval technology. Protocols vary from one information storage system to another.

Inherited Information

In a hierarchical descriptive system, information that applies to one level of data because it applies to a level above it in the hierarchy.

Intellectual Access

In a repository, the ability to know what materials meet the needs of the researcher.

Inventories

A basic archival finding aid. Inventories typically consist of hierarchical descriptions of the contents of a collection, starting with contextual information of the whole, then breaking out component series, subseries, and files.

ISAAR(CPF)

International Standard for Archival Authority Records for Corporations, Persons, and Families. A content standard for archival authority records developed by the ICA's Committee on Descriptive Standards.

ISAD(G)v2

Generalized International Standard for Archival Description. A set of data elements developed as a tool for standardizing archival description internationally by the Description Section of the ICA.

ISO

International Organization for Standardization. A network of national standards institutes from 148 countries working in partnership with international organizations, governments, industry, business, and consumer representatives in the development of technical standards.

LCNAF

Library of Congress Name Authority File. The largest collection of authorized names in North America, developed and supported by the Library of Congress.

LCSH

Library of Congress Subject Headings. The largest thesaurus of subject headings in North America, developed and supported by the Library of Congress. The terms reflect the holdings of the LC and include topics and geographical and organizational entities.

MAD

Manual of Archival Description. The British manual for archival description.

Manuscript Collection

A group of historical documents created by a person or family.

MARBI

Machine-Readable Bibliographic Information. An interdivisional committee of the American Library Association (ALA) charged with oversight of MARC.

MARC

Machine Readable Cataloging. A data structure for electronic storage and exchange of bibliographic information.

MARC-AMC

Machine Readable Cataloging–Archives and Manuscript Collections. A data structure for electronic storage and exchange of summary information on historical documents.

Markup Element

> Code and textual content within a marked up document (e.g., <markuptag>Textual content</markuptag>).

Markup Language

> A set of markup conventions used together for encoding text for electronic publication.

Markup Tag

> The code that sits at the beginning and end of the textual content. Tags will be either start tags (e.g., <markuptag>) or end tags (e.g., </markuptag>) .

MEP

> Model Editions Partnership. A ten-year research project at the University of South Carolina funded by the National Historical Records and Publications Commission to develop tools and protocols for electronic publication of historical documents.

Metadata

> An encoded description of a document or group of documents. EAD markup creates a metadata description of both the finding aid it describes and the collection described by the inventory.

NACO

> The name authority program component of the Program for Cooperative Cataloging at the Library of Congress. Through this program, participants contribute authority records for names, uniform titles, and series to the national authority file.

NISTF

> National Information Systems Task Force. An SAA committee investigating the role of information technology in archival description and access between 1981and1984, eventually recommending the development of a MARC format for archival description.

Normalize

> A process in the markup that uses an attribute in an element to standardize the content of the text the element describes (e.g., <date normal="1944-06-16">June 16, 1944</date>).

OPAC

> Online Public Access Catalog. A bibliographic database of institutional holdings.

Original Order

> The principle of archival arrangement that holds that materials should remain in the order created by the organization, individual, or family that created them.

Papers

> Archival materials generated by persons or families.

PCC

> Program for Cooperative Cataloging. An international cooperative effort lead by the Library of Congress to provide cost-effective cataloging that meets mutually-accepted standards of libraries around the world.

Physical Access

> In a repository, the ability to locate materials that researchers request.

Provenance

> 1) Information regarding the origins and custodial history of historical documents. 2) The principle that collections in a historical repository should not be intermingled.

RAD

> *Rules for Archival Description.* Canadian standard for archival description.

Records

> Archival materials generated by government or organizations.

Search Engine

> An information retrieval tool which matches a user's query statement with the content of an index of sources.

Series

> A component of an archival collection bound together by some common creator, function, form, era, etc.

Stylesheet

> The program which controls the appearance of an electronic document on the screen.

Subordinate Component

> In a hierarchical arrangement, a component which falls beneath another. Except for the collection level in archival description, every component in a hierarchical arrangement represents a subordinate component of the level above it.

TEI

Text Encoding Initiative. The protocol for encoding various humanities documents for electronic publication.

Template

An electronic "form" which hides much of the coding needed to create an electronically published document, thus making it possible for relatively lightly-trained staff to provide proper encoding of information.

TGN

Thesaurus of Geographic Names. A thesaurus developed by the J. Paul Getty Trust to support research into art, architecture, and material culture.

TOC

Table of contents. A navigational device in a published document.

Union Database or Catalog

A database or OPAC containing records describing the holdings of more than one repository.

VAN

Vermont Archival Network. An informal collaborative of small repositories in northern Vermont which developed ArcCat, a union database of their holdings.

Wrapper Tag

In a markup language, a tag or element that holds only other tags instead of text.

XML

Extensible Markup Language. A metalanguage for developing markup languages.

Bibliography

Books

Bellardo, Lewis J., and Lynn Lady Bellardo. *A Glossary for Archivists, Manuscript Curators, and Records Managers.* Chicago: Society of American Archivists, 1992.

Buel, Joy Day, and Richard Buel Jr. *The Way of Duty: A Woman and Her Family in Revolutionary America.* New York: Norton, 1984.

Bureau of Canadian Archivists. *Rules for Archival Description.* 3rd. ed. Burlington, Vt.: Gower, 2000.

Canadian Council of Archivists. *Rules for Archival Description.* Ottawa: Canadian Council of Archivists, 2003.

Conway, Paul. *Partners in Research: Improving Access to the Nation's Archive.* Pittsburgh: Archives and Museum Informatics, 1994.

Cook, Michael G. *The Management of Information from Archives.* 2nd ed. Brookfield, Vt.: Gower, 1999.

Crawford, Walt. *MARC for Library Use.* 23rd ed. Boston: G. K. Hall, 1989.

Describing Archives: A Content Standard. Chicago: Society of American Archivists, 2004.

FIAF Cataloguing Rules for Film Archives. Munich: K. G. Saur, 1991.

Fox, Michael, Peter Wilkerson, and Susan Warren. *Introduction to Archival Arrangement and Description: Access to Cultural Heritage.* Los Angeles: Getty Information Institute, 1998.

Haworth, Kent M. "Archival Description: Content and Context in Search of Structure." *Encoded Archival Description on the Internet.* Edited by Daniel V. Pitti and Wendy Duff. New York: Haworth, 2001.

Hensen, Steven L. "Archival Cataloging and the Internet: The Implications and Impact of EAD." *Encoded Archival Description on the Internet.* Edited by Daniel V. Pitti and Wendy Duff. New York: Haworth, 2001.

———. *Archives, Personal Papers, and Manuscripts: A Cataloging Manual for Archival Repositories.* Chicago: Society of American Archivists, 1998.

International Association of Sound and Audiovisual Archives. *IASA Cataloging Rules: A Manual for the Description of Sound Recordings and Related Audiovisual Media.* Stockholm: International Association of Sound and Audiovisual Archives, 1999.

Joint Steering Committee for Revision of the AACR. *Anglo-American Cataloging Rules.* Ottawa: Canadian Library Association; Chicago: American Library Association, 2002.

Miller, Frederic. *Arranging and Describing Archives and Manuscripts.* Chicago: Society of American Archivists, 1990.

Peterson, Toni, dir. *Art and Architecture Thesaurus.* 2nd ed. New York: Oxford University, 1994.

Porter, Vicki, and Robin Thornes. *A Guide to the Description of Architectural Drawings.* New York: G. K. Hall, 1994.

Proctor, Margaret, and Michael G. Cook. *Manual of Archival Description.* 3rd ed. Brookfield, Vt.: Gower, 2000.

Sample Forms for Archival and Records Management Programs. Lenexa, Kan., and Chicago: ARMA International and the Society of American Archivists, 2002.

Stibbe, Hugo, Vivien Cartmell, and Velma Parker, eds. *Cartographic Materials: A Manual of Interpretation for AACR2.* Ottawa: Canadian Library Association, 1982.

Thesaurus of Graphic Materials. Washington, D.C.: Library of Congress, 1995.

White-Hensen, Wendy. *Archival Moving Image Materials: A Cataloging Manual.* 2nd. ed. Washington, D.C.: Library of Congress, 2000.

Journal Articles

Dooley, Jackie M. et al. "Encoded Archival Description, Part 1: Context and Theory." *American Archivist* 60 (1997): 264–354.

———. "Encoded Archival Description, Part 2: Case Studies." *American Archivist* 60 (1997): 370–455.

Eppard, Philip B., ed. "Special Section: Users and Archival Research." *American Archivist* 66 (2003): 9–101.

Hensen, Steven L. "'NISTF II' and EAD: The Evolution of Archival Description." *American Archivist* 60 (1997): 286.

Meissner, Dennis. "First Things First: Re-engineering Finding Fids for the Implementation of EAD." *American Archivist* 60 (1997): 372–387.

Pitti, Daniel V. "Encoded Archival Description: The Development of an Encoding Standard for Archival Finding Aids." *American Archivist* 60 (1997): 268–283.

Prom, Christopher J. "Does EAD Play Well with Other Metadata Standards? Searching and Retrieving Using the OAI Protocols." *Journal of Archival Organization* 1, no. 3 (2002): 51–72.

Redding, Clay. "Reengineering Finding Aids Revisited: Current Archival Description Practice and Its Effect on EAD Implementation." *Journal of Archival Organization* 1, no. 3 (2002): 35–50.

Websites

California Digital Library. "Online Archive of California." Web page, 2003 [accessed January 2004]. Available at www.oac.cdlib.org/.

Canadian Council of Archives. "Canadian Council of Archives." Web page, 2003 [accessed January 2004]. Available at www.cdncouncilarchives.ca/archdesrules.html.

Catalog of Vermont Archives and Manuscripts. "ArcCat: Vermont Archives and Manuscripts." Web page, 2000 [accessed January 2004]. Available at arccat.uvm.edu.

Council on Library and Information Resources. "Scholarship, Instruction, and Libraries at the Turn of the Century." Web page, 1999 [accessed January 2004]. Available at www.clir.org/pubs/reports/pub78/pub78.pdf.

Cover, Robin. "Encoded Archival Context." Web page [accessed January 2004]. Available at xml.coverpages.org/eac.html.

———. "ISO 8601 Date Codes." Web page [accessed January 2004]. Available at xml.coverpages.org/ISO-FDIS-8601.pdf.

EAD Roundtable of the Society of American Archivists. "EAD Help Pages EAD Cookbook." Web page, 2003 [accessed January 2004]. Available at jefferson.village.virginia.edu/ead/cookbookhelp.html.

Everson, Michael. "Script Codes ISO 15924." Web page, 2003 [accessed January 2004]. Available at www.evertype.com/standards/iso15924.

Fox, Michael, Peter Wilkerson, and Susan Warren. "Introduction to Archival Arrangement and Description: Access to Cultural Heritage." Web page [accessed January 2004]. Available at www.schistory.org/getty.

Historical Manuscripts Commission. "ISAAR(CPF)." Web page, 2004 [accessed January 2004]. Available at www.hmc.gov.uk/icacds/eng/ISAAR(CPF)2.pdf.

International Council on Archives. "ICA." Web page, 2004 [accessed January 2004]. Available at www.ica.org/.

International Standards Organization. "ISO3166 Country Codes." Web page, 2003 [accessed January 2004]. Available at www.iso.ch/iso/en/prods-services/iso3166ma/02iso-3166-code-list/list-en1.html.

J. Paul Getty Trust. "Art and Architecture Thesaurus (Research at the Getty)." Web page [accessed January 2004]. Available at www.getty.edu/research/tools/vocabulary/aat.

J. Paul Getty Trust. "Getty Thesaurus of Geographic Names (Research at the Getty)." Web page, 2003 [accessed January 2004]. Available at www.getty.edu/research/conducting_research/vocabularies/tgn/.

Library of Congress. "Codes for the Representation of Names of Languages." Web page, 2003 [accessed January 2004]. Available at www.loc.gov/standards/iso639-2/englangn.html.

Library of Congress. "Division of the World." Web page, 2003 [accessed January 2004]. Available www.loc.gov/catdir/pcc/saco/alpha405.html.

Library of Congress. "Library of Congress Authorities." Web page, 2002 [accessed January 2004]. Available at authorities.loc.gov.

Library of Congress. "MARC Code List for Organizations." Web page, 2004 [accessed January 2004]. Available at www.loc.gov/marc/organizations/orgshome.html.

Library of Congress. "Program for Cooperative Cataloging." Web page, 2003 [accessed January 2004]. Available at loc.gov/catdir/pcc/2001pcc.html.

Library of Congress. "Program for Cooperative Cataloging Annual Report 2003." Web page, 2003 [accessed January 2004]. Available at loc.gov/catdir/pcc/annualrpt03.html.

Research Library Group. "RLG and Access to Primary Sources." Web page, 2003 [accessed January 2004]. Available at www.rlg.org/primary/index.html.

Research Library Group. "RLG Archival Resources." Web page, 2002 [accessed January 2004]. Available at www.rlg.org/arr/index.html.

Research Library Group. "RLG EAD Best Practice Guidelines." Web page, 2003 [accessed January 2004]. Available at www.rlg.org/rlgead/eadguides.html.

Research Library Group. "RLG SAA 2002 Forum: Metadata Matters: RLG Update on Current Metadata Initiatives." Web page, 2002 [accessed January 2004]. Available at www.rlg.org/events/metadata2002/.

Society of American Archivists. "Encoded Archival Description Tag Library." Web page, 2002 [accessed January 2004]. Available at www.loc.gov/ead/tglib/appendix_d.html.

Society of American Archivists. "Society of American Archivists." Web page, 2003 [accessed January 2004]. Available at www.archivists.org.

Unpublished Work

Engst, Elaine. "Standard Elements for the Description of Archives and Manuscript Collections; A Report to the Society of American Archivists Task Force on National Information Systems." 1980. Photocopy in the possession of the author.

Riggs, Michelle. "Correlation of Demand for EAD in the Job Market and Graduate Archival Education." 2003. Independent study in the School of Library and Information Science, Louisiana State University, completed fall, 2003.

E-mail

Whitfield, Gregory, RLG Product Manager. E-mail message to the author, November 23, 2004.

Index

About the Author

Elizabeth Dow, then public services librarian in Special Collections at the University of Vermont, saw Daniel Pitti's 1995 demonstration of EAD at the SAA Meeting in Washington, D.C. It excited her so that she had to literally walk around the block a couple of times to absorb the implications of the technology she had just seen.

Back at UVM and in league with Hope Greenberg of Academic Computing Services, she wrote a grant proposal which brought SGML software to campus. With it she launched UVM's EAD initiative. By December 2000, she had published over 120 EAD marked-up inventories. She tells the tale in "EAD and the Small Repository," *American Archivist* 60 (Fall 1997), 446-455.

Dow holds a Ph.D. in library science from the University of Pittsburgh and teaches the archives track in the School of Library and Information Science at Louisiana State University.